PRAY
PRICE *the*

About the Author

Having served as a United Methodist pastor for twenty-eight years, Dr. Terry Teykl is currently traveling full time teaching and training in the area of prayer. His desire is to motivate and equip local churches to join the surge of prayer evangelism that is sweeping the globe. With wisdom, practicality and humor, he urges Christians of all denominations to unite in prayer aimed at the Great Commission.

Dr. Teykl resides in Houston, Texas with his wife Kay. They have four grown children and five grandchildren. He is the author of several books, including: *Making Room to Pray, Personal Prayer Evangelism, Your Pastor: Preyed On or Prayed For, Healing in the Bible, Acts Twenty-Nine*, and has also developed a wide array of other practical prayer helps.

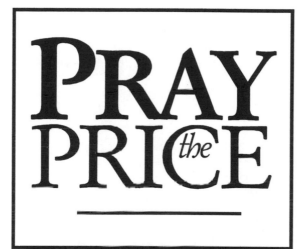

Dr. Terry Teykl

Prayer Point Press

Pray the Price

Prayer Point Press
2100 N. Carrolton Dr.
Muncie, Indiana 47304

Phone: 765 759-0215
To order, call toll-free: 1-888-656-6067

Table of Contents

Dedication

This book is dedicated to the Reverend and Mrs. Joe Young who believed in me and helped me get started as a United Methodist Pastor.

Preface

One morning at 3:00 a.m., I heard a loud knock on the parsonage door. With a torn shirt, messy hair, and a red face, one of my church members asked if he could come in. He and his wife had been fighting, as they did quite often, but on that night the man was particularly distraught.

"We've been to every counselor in town and none of them helped," he said. "And if anyone gives us another book to read, I'll scream! We—I need something more."

I often think of that incident because I believe that hurting, frustrated husband spoke the heart need of all of us. More than a self-help book, a great sermon, or any other efforts of man, what he needed so desperately was a touch from God. He knew that one divine encounter with the creator of the universe could turn things around for him and his wife.

As I hear the cries from within our beloved United Methodist Church, I know that what we need goes beyond sermons, hymnals, polity and structure.

We have tried so many other solutions which have produced limited results; could it be that we need to humble ourselves before God and invite His presence into our midst? Like the man who had given up on every other possible remedy, I believe we simply need a sovereign touch for a spiritual awakening.

For the last ten years, my passion has been for prayer evangelism. I see whole denominations mobilizing to pray, and even whole cities establishing prayer ministries. In light of this prayer epidemic, I sense more than ever before that God is calling us as a denomination to pray a new price. Although spiritual solutions can be fraught with extremes and subjective misinterpretations, we are nevertheless born of the Spirit, filled with the Spirit, and perhaps even renewed by the Spirit.

I do not think God is finished with the United Methodist Church—I think He wants to do a new thing in us and through us. He is sounding an alarm to awaken us to what He is doing in the earth today. If we will pray, surely He will pour out His love to us in a powerful new way.

Our goal is to enlist thousands of United Methodists to pray every week for such an awakening. In 200 years of existence, no such call has ever been made. Although it must go forth through clay vessels, this is not the call of men. It did not originate in United Methodist factions or camps and is not simply a fleeting whim of some particular theological bias. Rather, this call comes from above and it is our role to recognize and respond to it. It is a move of God that is bigger than, but not to the exclusion of, these people called Methodists. Let us pray!

1

Awaken the
Sleeping Giant

The pavement was hot in Seville, Spain. The smell and feel of death still lingered in the air from the day before when crackling flames, "to the glory of God," had consumed nearly one hundred heretics in a "splendid act of faith." As the "tortured, suffering people, sunk in iniquity," shuffled about the streets, they all recognized Him, and "flocked about Him." He moved among them silently, with a "gentle smile of infinite compassion." He blessed them. This was not the return that He promised to make at the end of time when He walked the earth fifteen centuries ago; He was visiting His children for only a moment during this terrible time of the inquisition.

As the children threw flowers before Him and cried, "Hosannah," the weeping mourners brought to Him a little, open, white coffin which held a girl of seven years. The crowd shouted to the crying mother,

"He will raise your child!" She threw herself at His
feet and stretched out her hands to Him, and He looked
on her with compassion. "Maiden, arise!" he said, and
she sat up in the coffin, still holding a bunch of white
roses they had put in her hands.

But at that same moment, the cardinal himself—
the Grand Inquisitor—had passed. As Jesus was led
away by the guards, the people bowed in trembling
obedience and submission, not to Him, but to the
powerful, old inquisitor.

In the "close, gloomy vaulted prison in the An-
cient palace of the Holy Inquisition," Jesus sat waiting.
Having been locked up on the charge of heresy, He
refused to speak. The inquisitor came to Him and said,
"...Thou hast no right to add anything to what Thou
hadst said of old. Why, then, art Thou come to hinder
us? ...But tomorrow I shall condemn Thee and burn
Thee at the stake as the worst of heretics. And the
very people who have today kissed Thy feet, tomorrow at the faintest sign from me will rush to heap up
the embers of Thy fire." Jesus only listened. After
some time, He "approached the old man in silence
and softly kissed him on the forehead. That was his
answer."

This scene, so powerfully created in Fyodor
Dostoyevsky's *The Brothers Karamazov*, could be rewritten in some form to fit any period in history. The
church had become so "efficient" that Jesus no longer
fit into the agenda. They did not want Him around
attracting attention or interfering with their plans. He
was no longer the focus; in fact, He had become a
nuisance. Somehow, as the church had become an

organized, functioning body, its very lifeline had been cut.

Recycling

Let us not forget—the history of Israel reflects a repeated tendency of God's people to fall back into their old ways and lose perspective of their desperate need for Him. We see this pattern throughout the Old Testament. The Israelites were called to leave Egypt, and cross the Jordan. They were established as a nation and people of God, and enjoyed a time of great prosperity. Then national pride set in. The Israelites fell away from God, forgetting that it was He who had given them all they had. Their success drew them away from their need for His manifest presence. But, God, in His infinite mercy, sent a prophetic messenger to call His people back. When they turned and returned, judgment was spared.

Richard Niebur traced this same cycle of the church in His book *Social Sources of Denominationalism*. He explains that God calls us in the Gospel to leave the old life of sin and self, and cross in baptism to be His people, His church. We are to reflect His glory. Inevitably, the revival soon develops into a sect, the sect becomes a church, and seminaries are built to preserve the traditions. Then the church becomes an institution which eventually becomes an end in itself, and things close down and petrify. Maintenance and self-preservation become the order of the day, and everything exists for the sake of the institution. Like a giant factory turning out a product, day after day, each worker does his job and nothing else. Creativity and imagination that might produce change are forbidden for fear that productivity might be slowed down or that the "product" might be altered. Risk takers are pushed out. Visions and dreams are discouraged unless sanctioned by headquarters. Pastors become spiritual clones who are trained only to keep the machine running smoothly. Blind loyalty to the party line is demanded, and cautious, politically correct actions replace bold, innovative plans that could bear much fruit.

Dead End for the Mainline?

An article appeared in the August 9, 1993 edition of *Newsweek* magazine that caught my attention with the title, "Dead End For the Mainline?" The article contained some very telltale statistics revealing a bleak outlook for mainline churches. The author cited membership figures for 1965 and for 1992 for what he called "liberal Protestantism's seven sister denominations—the Episcopal Church, the Presbyterian Church (U.S.A.), the American Baptist Churches, the United Church of Christ, the Christian Church (Disciples of Christ), the Evangelical Lutheran church in America, and the United Methodist Church. Each of these institutions showed a decline in membership over that period of time. The losses were staggering, some denominations withering in size by almost fifty percent! If added together, the numbers showed that these seven churches, over the last 30 years, have seen 6.9 million people leave their flocks for other pastures. The article stated that they who once "helped define America and its values," are now "struggling to define themselves in a world where adjectives like 'Methodist' or 'Presbyterian' no longer mean anything to most Americans."

It would be very presumptuous on our part to think that as United Methodists, we are exempt from the patterns of God's people. We began as a great revival, we were a sect, we became a great church, and we stand as an institution. Could it be that now our United Methodist Church, as well as other mainline denominations, are in a crisis of money and membership, identity and loyalty, because we have lost our passion for Jesus and His mandate to fulfill the Great Commission? Could it be that we are losing 50,000 members each year because our once fervent dependence on God has been replaced by vain self-sufficiency? Are we sleepwalking through the motions of conducting services and processing liturgies—merely dreaming of new plans that might spark awakening? Do we still have the Father's heart to reach this generation for Christ?

Bred for Success

Although the *Newsweek* article seemed discouraging, I did find it interesting to note that the author stated with confidence, "Mainline Protestants were bred for bigger things." Yes! He explained that after the Civil War, the mainline denominations developed into "large, bureaucratic national corporations." He says:

> In addition to controlling their own foreign and domestic missions, denominations produced Sunday-

school curricula, hymnals and other products that they marketed to local congregations. They also credentialed ministers and ran colleges. By the middle of this century, the corporate denominations were the most prominent feature of American Protestantism. Politicians heeded their leaders, and the circulation of journals like the now defunct *Presbyterian Life* almost matched *Newsweek's.*

All seven of the Protestant churches he referred to, especially the United Methodists, are institutional giants. As a denomination, we have much to be proud of: two hundred years in existence, 37,000 churches representing virtually every county in America, a reputation for advocating the plight of the poor and the social gospel, billions of dollars in property, ownership of colleges, universities, orphanages and hospitals, twelve seminaries, and over eight million members. With regard to size, stability, tradition and resources, few institutions are more equipped to effect world-wide change of any kind than the United Methodist Church. Although many have written us off as a dying breed, I believe that if this giant awakes, it will once again become a leader in fulfilling the Great Commission. I believe God could even use this denomination to help bring about an unprecedented revival in the land.

But first we need a spiritual awakening among these people called United Methodists, and I believe a united prayer effort is the key. If we can enlist even ten percent of our denomination to pray a new price, it would open the doors and windows so that the fresh wind of the Spirit could blow through our Sunday school classes, our board meetings, our outreach efforts, and our morning services. We could experience God in a new way.

Wake-Up Call

As a United Methodist pastor for twenty-eight years, I am convinced that our denomination and our people are desperate for a fresh outpouring of God's power. We need a wake-up call! More radical than reorganizing our polity, more extreme than adopting a new hymnal, our solution may be a return to our Weslyan heritage of tenacious prayer evangelism. Never before in our history have we had a national call to prayer in the Methodist movement; we are long overdue. Any other solution that excludes a renewed commitment to prayer is like shifting the chairs around on the deck of the Titanic. We may change the appearance, but the ship is still going down.

Radical Dependence

God has placed prayer in the scheme of things in a very unique way. In all His power and sovereignty, He has chosen prayer as the means for His interaction with His people. Jesus himself, in addition to teaching often about prayer, modeled it as a radical dependence on the Father for everything. He prayed to know God, to know His will, to have power to do that will, and to have perseverance to finish His course. Even for Jesus, prayer was the very source of life in every circumstance.

In fact, I would even say that prayer is the outward, visible manifestation of a wonderful dependency on the creator of the universe. In Him we are marvelously wrapped up, and without Him we can not live. We look to Him, live for Him and are unhappy without Him. When we are dependent on God, we need daily contact with Him, and prayer is that point of contact. No matter our situation, we look to Him for meaning, direction and resources. We are content as long as we are living in Him and through Him. This is by far the healthiest dependency known to mankind. Anything less than this intense reliance on the Father leaves us searching for something to substitute in His place. But we are made to depend on Him alone, so no substitute will suffice. Paul summed it up in Acts 17:28, "For in Him we live and move and have our being."

Through prayer, God is able to bless His people and their mission. Without it, spiritual awakening will never come. Jesus said, "Ask and it will be given to you, seek and you will find, knock and the door will be opened to you. For everyone who asks receives, he who seeks finds, and to him who knocks the door will be opened." He adds, "Which of you fathers, if your son asks for a fish, will give him a stone instead? Or if he asks for an egg, will give him a scorpion? If you then, though you are evil, know how to give good gifts to your children, how much more will your Father in heaven give the Holy Spirit to those who ask Him?" (Luke 11:9-13)

Prayer is simply asking God to help us. In fact, James says, "You do not have because you do not ask" (James 4:2). No matter how many resources we own, or how much ability we feel we have, we must continually go before God and ask for His guidance and help. We need His blessing and heart in all that we do so that we avoid the pitfall of man-centered agendas. If we will ask Him to awaken our church, He will do it to make a name for His Son.

When Luke tells us to seek, the inference is that we must be diligent, not allowing ourselves to be distracted by anything. To seek is to press into God with all our heart, soul and strength for His will to be done. It means we must persevere past all forms of resistance. So many Christians determine to pray about something, but then give up when God does not respond fast enough or when He responds in some unexpected way. In our ready-made, microwave society, it seems we have a hard time learning how to be tenacious about anything, especially prayer. But I believe that persistence can turn the heart of God.

The promise of prayer is that if we continually knock, doors will open to reveal new vistas and opportunities. When we ask and seek, God answers us by opening our eyes to see new revelations, ideas, visions and hopes. The more we knock, the more doors He can open and make available to us.

The Father's Heart

It is important to understand that this is a call, not just to prayer, but to prayer evangelism. It is a call to prayer with a specific, driving purpose. Simply stirring up more prayer ministries will not result in an awakening unless they are aimed at bringing new converts into the Kingdom.

During one of our Schools of Prayer earlier this year, I held up a poster of a missing child, and I told a story of a man I know whose seven year old son disappeared several years ago, never to be found. As we all identified with the unspeakable pain that plagues that father's heart, I explained that our heavenly Father also grieves over his lost children. He desires that none should perish, but that all would find salvation. He yearns for His kids to come home. Although I know that God hears and answers all of our prayers, I imagine that when we utter a prayer for one of these precious ones, it registers like a 911 call in heaven. A life is on the line. We never need to wonder about what God's will is with regard to salvation. We can pray with boldness, because we are praying His heart.

As I travel around America, I find that in almost every city, between seventy and eighty percent of the population is unchurched. That means that in a city with 100,000 people, on any given Sunday morning, 70,000 to 80,000 of them are somewhere other than church. While on a four month sabbatical, I discovered where many of them migrate to while we worship. I visited all kinds of places during typical church hours and saw first hand that Wal-Mart is packed, recreational areas such as parks and lakes are humming with activity, and local pancake houses have people lined up out the door. I even went to a Frisbee-catching contest for dogs and stood watching with hundreds of other spectators! And there was really no way to count the number of people I saw washing their cars, mowing their lawns, or cleaning out their garages. After many years in ministry, it really dawned on me that when we sit down in church on Sunday mornings, we are in the minority. A large percentage of our population could not be any less interested in what goes on behind our stained glass windows.

We need a spiritual awakening in our United Methodist Church not to save the institution, but to save the lost. For it is in bringing people into relationship with Jesus for the first time that we will truly experience all God has to offer. There is no more intimate encounter with our heavenly Father than when we bring one of His children home.

Prayer Evangelism

Not only is it time for a united call to a new era of prayer, but I believe more specifically that prayer evangelism is the order of the day.

Prayer evangelism is the term I use to describe praying with a burden for the unchurched. It means to pray that the eyes of the blind would be opened to see the love of Jesus and the meaning of the cross. It means to target the Great Commission in prayer so as to win this generation to Christ.

This type of prayer is already surging across the globe in other countries such as Korea, Argentina, Brazil and India, and is finding its way to cities in America such as Colorado Springs and Pittsburgh. The models of prayer evangelism are manifold. Believers of all denominations are engaging in bold, new creative forms of prayer for their unsaved loved ones, neighborhoods, and cities. In fact, C. Peter Wagner, noted author and teacher on prayer, says that prayer has reached "epidemic proportions" in this generation.

A Match Made in Heaven

Prayer evangelism is by no means a new concept. In fact, the two were meant to be together from the start. The book of Acts chronicles example after example of how the two are intertwined. In fact, I think it is safe to say that one of the primary functions of prayer in the Kingdom of God is to bring people to the point of salvation.

Look at Acts 16. Verses 13 and 14 read, "On the Sabbath we went outside the city gate to the river, where we expected to find a place of prayer. We sat down and began to speak to the women who had gathered there. One of those listening was a woman named Lydia.... The Lord opened her heart to respond to Paul's message." In the next scene, we read, "Once when we were going to the place of prayer, we were met by a slave girl..." (v. 16). Several verses later, we find that the girl who was troubled is set free and evidently receives the gospel. Verses 22 through 34 tell the story of how Paul and Silas made a prayer room out of their jail cell, and then shared Christ with the jailer. He asks them, "Sirs, what must I do to be saved?" "Believe in the Lord Jesus, and you will be saved—you and your household" (vs. 30-31), they replied. And the jailer and all his family were immediately baptized.

Acts is the story of things happening as the disciples were going to pray, while they were praying, and after they prayed. In just one chapter, three examples of prayer yielded three examples of evangelism. For the apostles in the early church, prayer evangelism was the very essence of life.

The Great Divorce

Unfortunately, somewhere along the way as the church developed and made tremendous strides in organization and resources, prayer and evangelism grew apart and eventually separated, each one going its own way. Prayer became listless; it had no list of the lost. It became visionless; it lost sight of those who were unsaved. It was lame; it could not even meet church members' needs. It was tame; it set no captives free. Prayer married itself off to self-serving attitudes and man-centered agendas.

Evangelism, on the other hand, was in trouble as well. It gave in to hard-sell tactics, marketing techniques and advertising schemes. It became programmatic, turning out memorized presentations of a gospel turned academic. It bought into methods and turned them into sales campaigns. When it could not produce converts, it settled for producing good attendance or starting a scouting troop. When it could not generate professions of faith, it was happy just to "get them in the building."

The two, once so intimately bound together, have suffered and struggled along on their own. But the real victims are the children—lost children who need to be brought home. The ones who are suffering are the hundreds and thousands of unbelievers who are desperate for hope and salvation, and it is for their sake that we must bring prayer and evangelism back together.

Remarriage

The good news is that all over the world, prayer and evangelism are being reunited with unprecedented passion. The United Prayer Track has mobilized 36 million people to pray for one hundred gateway cities in unevangelized nations. Harvest Evangelism, founded by Ed Silvoso and fueled by his book *That None Should Perish*, has launched city-wide prayer evangelism strategies in hundreds of cities. *Pray USA!*, which is a prayer initiative of Mission America, will launch thirty days of prayer and fasting in April of 1997. *Houses of Prayer Everywhere* is planting prayer cells in neighborhoods and workplaces all over the country to pray for neighbors, friends and co-workers who need to know Jesus. We are seeing the best of prayer married to the best of evangelism for genuine results.

Praying or Just Paying

In many ways, the United Methodists have paid prices to be a great church. In 1994, our local congregations gave a staggering $3,430,351,778—just under 3.5 billion dollars—for everything from building maintenance to ministerial support to operating expenses. Of that total, over $100 million was given toward benevolence funds to help those in need. As clergy, we paid dearly in time and talent to acquire educational credentials. We have paid the price in taking bold stands against all forms of injustice and social inequalities. All this is commendable.

But as a denomination, are we praying the price? Are we joined across the nation in a united prayer effort to affect our cities for Christ? In the midst of our identity crisis, are we praying for a renewed vision of Jesus and a renewed sense of purpose? In our local churches, how many of our members are committed to ongoing prayer ministries? How many of our churches are seeing professions of faith on a regular basis? How much time is spent in the monthly preachers' meeting in prayer? At our Annual Conferences, are our leaders setting aside prolonged periods of time to ask, seek and knock?

The one thing Jesus desired for the church was that it be a "house of prayer" (Matthew 21:13), not a house of worship services, or a house of day care, or even a house of outreach programs. All these things, worthy as they are, must never be allowed to squeeze out the most important, powerful, life-changing, soul-winning thing we can do as a church. John Wesley believed that God does nothing except in answer to prayer, so if we are to accomplish anything of eternal value, we must do it from our knees.

The Fatal Blow

In the heat of World War II, the Germans worked fervently behind closed doors constructing what they thought would be the greatest military weapon ever conceived. In mid 1941, they launched the battleship Bismarck, with an armored shell eighteen inches thick, and a gun that could hurl a shell the size of a Volkswagen over twenty miles. They were convinced that it could destroy the entire British navy and that its supreme power would quickly afford a German victory. Almost immediately, the floating fortress sank one of the highly feared British battleships called the Hood, striking fear in the hearts of her equals. The Bismarck seemed impenetrable.

But not long after its impressive debut, the ultimate German weapon was spotted by a pair of enemy sea planes on patrol. Made partially of canvas, the planes carried only one torpedo each, since they were not designed to be aggressive attack planes. But as the planes flew over the battleship, they both fired their torpedoes. The first one hit the side of the Bismarck and exploded, but did no damage. Similarly, the second hit the tail of the ship and bounced off, exploding in the water but doing no visible damage. The planes fled quickly, not wishing to exchange fire. But little did they know that the second torpedo had, in fact, knocked the rudder of the Bismarck off its hinges, and without a rudder, the mighty fortress was left with no way to steer. Although the damage seemed totally insignificant, the most powerful, indestructible, military force ever created was actually helpless in the water. Within hours, it had floated directly into the middle of a British fleet, which shelled it again and again until the great ship went down.

The Church's Rudder

I believe prayer is the rudder of the United Methodist Church. Without it, we have no sense of direction and no ability to steer. We may have an inspired vision, abundant resources, good location and a computer loaded with UMIS, yet without prayer we are left at the mercy of every religious fad or trend.

I simply offer this book as a plea to United Methodists to pray a new price. Isaiah 43:18-19 says, "Forget the former things, do not dwell on the past. See I am doing a new thing. Now it springs up. Do you not perceive it?" God is doing a new thing today all across the world and we need not be left out! A united prayer effort could open the doors for us to not only perceive what God is doing, but also receive a new and fresh outpouring of His Holy Spirit to reach cities for Him.

Study Questions

1. What does it mean to "shift the chairs around on the deck of the Titanic?" Can you identify ways in which your church or the UMC at large has done this?

2. What methods do you notice churches in your city using to attract members? How effective do you think they are?

3. What are some substitutes we put in place of prayer as a church body? What takes the place of prayer in your personal life?

4. Have you ever experienced a spiritual awakening? Describe what sparked it, how it felt, and what the results were.

5. Who are some of the unreached people where you live? Can you imagine a dynamic move of God happening among those people? What might spark such an awakening?

2

Pray the Price:
A Definition

To awaken this sleeping giant called United Methodism, we need to enlist an unrelenting army of men, women, youth and pastors who will stand against the forces of disunity that tend to divide us. I know God is pleased when men come together in prayer and submission. When women intercede in harmony, they can move mountains! Concerted prayer by young people is powerful and effective. And when pastors and church leaders pray together with one heart and purpose, they are praying a price for awakening that can not be had anywhere else.

One of the primary mission statements of our ministry is to "target the Great Commission in prayer so that by praying the price we might win this generation to Christ." But what do we mean by "praying the price"? What does it mean in regard to renewal, evangelism, and winning our cities? Can prayer really impact a local high school, street-wise gangs, crime rates, and the moral makeup of a city? Can prayer alone bring people out of darkness into the Kingdom of light? I am not only convinced that it can do all of these things, but I see it happening all over America, in towns and cities of every shape and size. Ed Silvoso, a premier teacher and author on the subject, says, "Prayer is not part of evangelism; prayer *is* evangelism." In other words, prayer is not just a contributing factor, it is the deciding factor.

Praying the price is not something that you can do one day and not the next. It is not simply a program that can be implemented or a recipe that can be followed. Rather, praying the price is a way of life. It is a paradigm, or a mindset, that governs every decision we make and every action we take. In short, it means, "Get out of the driver's seat and let God be God."

In this chapter, I want to share with you eight keys that define what it means to pray the price. For us as a denomination and as individual churches, it will be a journey, not just a one-time event that we plan at the next staff meeting and have catered to draw in a crowd. It will, in fact, require sacrifice, work and humility. It may stretch our religious comfort zone and challenge some of our patterns of thought and action. We will have to be willing to surrender ourselves completely to becoming a part of the new thing God is doing in the earth today. The rewards will only be as great as the investment.

Theology of Prayer

First, I believe we need to take a long, hard look at our theology of prayer. What do we really believe about it?

I heard a story once about a circus tight rope walker who was so daring and yet so steady that he amazed audiences at every performance. As part of his act, he pushed a wheel barrow loaded with chickens across the wire. One night, after pushing the cart safely to the platform on the other side to the roaring approval of the crowd, he asked for a volunteer to take the chickens' place. A hush fell in the big top. Although probably every person there would have enthusiastically agreed that the performer was so capable that he would never slip, actually getting out of their seat and climbing the tall ladder was a different matter all together!

Most people who read this book would probably say without hesitation that prayer is very important and it is at the heart of all we do. However, Peter Wagner is right on target when he speaks of the way we sometimes confuse rhetoric with action. We may speak favorably about prayer, but the reality is that we have no money in the budget devoted to it, no room in the building set aside for it, few small groups that spend any prolonged time doing it, and very little emphasis on it in our services or at our altars. If we were put on trial for being a praying church, I am afraid there would not be enough evidence to convict! It has occurred to me that perhaps the reason we talk so much and do so little is that we are in a crisis of belief as to the actual effectiveness of our prayers. If we really believed prayer worked, wouldn't we be beating a path to the throne weekly, daily, even hourly?

We know what John Wesley believed about prayer. For Wesley, every good thing began with prayer, was sustained by prayer, and finished by prayer. He practiced daily this radical dependence on God. It undergirded everything he did. In his book *The Devotional Life in the Wesleyan Spirit*, Steve Harper writes, "For Wesley, the chief instituted means of grace was prayer. It could be said that he lived to pray and prayed to live. He called prayer 'the grand means of drawing near to God.' Prayer had this importance because Wesley understood the Christian faith as a life lived in relationship with God through Jesus Christ. Because this is so, prayer was the key to maintaining that relationship." Because Wesley prayed the price, all of England was touched by God.

We also know that we are all part of a Church that was defined and formed through the committed prayers of its founders. They prayed a magnificent price. In addition, every church building that bears the United Methodist flame was erected by the fervent prayers of saints who had a vision. They were started in prayer, bathed in prayer, and built by resources won through prayer. Our churches today are the legacies of those who prayed a dear price for us to be here. Can we pray any less?

I believe we need to repent of our prayerlessness, turn in our substitutes and radically depend on Him. Our success will not hinge on our education or location. It will not come as a result of our ordination or experience. We will not win people to Jesus because of our name, our title, our management skills or our software package. Our success will be only as great as our reliance on God. We do not need more books (except maybe this one), more ideas or more committees. What we need is a fresh outpouring of God's power on us, our church, our district and our conference.

Can we repent of board meetings where we talk so much and pray so little? Could we consider praying more at men's breakfasts and eating less?

To pray the price is to formulate a viable, live theology of prayer that we live with and base our church activities on. To pray the price is to hammer this out in such a creative way that it is something real and meaningful. To pray the price is more than just quoting verses and then saying that is what we believe; it is a statement for ourselves and our church about prayer that makes it come alive in Biblical understanding and our historical context.

Seek a Vision

If we are going to pray a new price, we must have a vision, because prayer and vision are marvelously interrelated. Vision is the pulley designed to lift prayer off the dock of mundane, religious routine. They feed on each other, each drawing us closer and tighter to the heart of God and His purpose. Prayer without vision is mechanical, and vision without prayer is directionless and short-lived.

As a United Methodist pastor, I thought my primary purpose was to pay the apportionments so I could someday be assigned to a bigger church and get a larger salary package. But after eleven years of pastoring rural churches, I was assigned to start a new church with only eight people in a college town that was largely unchurched. Standing on a hill outside that city, as I was praying for people to come to know Jesus, God at that moment superceded my institutional goals with a goal to bring people into His Kingdom. He gave me a vision of evangelism as a way of life—church life, that is—and every decision we made from then on was governed by that vision.

Shortly after, He gave me a word, "Build the church in prayer." For me, the two connected. Prayer would continue to be everything it had been, but suddenly the back door of my prayer closet had been opened to reveal a world of evangelistic opportunity. God blessed that Aldersgate United Methodist Church with many professions of faith.

Praying the price is to make the connection between prayer and evangelism, and to build on that foundation a vision and plan for reaching your city. Walt Kallestad had such a vision for a unique Lutheran church reaching the city of Phoenix. As he prayed in a hotel room in Dallas, Texas, the Lord gave him a vision for reaching the lost through prayer evangelism. He went to Phoenix and planted the vision in the desert and watered it with prayer. He hired a man named Bjorn Pedersen to form a college of prayer alongside the church to train and equip people to pray. As a result of his vision, the Community of Joy Lutheran Church has grown dramatically and has had a tremendous impact not only in Phoenix, but across the country.

Another man who received a bold vision from God was a struggling pastor in a poor section of Seoul Korea. Wrapped in blankets to fend against the cold, he sat praying in his home—a small tent near the fledgling church where he preached. As he prayed, God showed him a vision of winning the lost through prayer evangelism and the power of the Holy Spirit. God revealed to him that he could bring about revival in a nation and win thousands of people to Christ if he would pray the price.

As he came "unwrapped," he became passionate to fulfill the Great Commission. He became single-minded about prayer and evangelism, and he purposed to see prayer become *the* work of the church. He launched a massive prayer evangelism thrust that landed on well-known prayer mountain, and set a precedent for others to follow. Today, Pastor David Cho leads the largest church in the world that continues to see people coming to Jesus as a result of persistent, committed intercession.

When we pray, I believe we enable God to give us divine glimpses of where He wants to take us. We can choose to muddle along under our own power and design, implementing the latest programs and working to meet the weekly budget, or we can ask God to show us His charted course and we can travel in His caravan. Why spend our lives on a muddy beach in

Matagorda, Texas when we could be on an airplane to the Caribbean?

In Acts 10, Peter went to the roof of the house to pray, and he fell into a trance. As he slept, he saw a vision of a sheet being lowered full of "ham sandwiches," food that was forbidden by law for the Jews to eat. But God told him, "Get up Peter. Eat" (v. 13). That vision eventually led him to the home of Cornelius, a Roman centurion, where he preached and the door to the Gentile world was opened. Peter took a course that he never would have, or even could have, had he not first received the vision from God.

Develop a Plan

To pray the price is to develop a well-defined prayer plan that will yield long term results. Having a solid theology is a good foundation, and receiving a vision is exciting, but we can not stop there.

Years ago I learned the difference between inspirational prayer and perspirational prayer. Inspirational prayer happens when we are inspired to pray by a moving sermon, a heart-warming appeal or an immediate crisis. It is event oriented and emotionally driven. Because this type of prayer tends to be based on feelings, it is also usually short lived since the desire to pray fades away as the emotion of the moment wears off. Of course, praying in response to a situation or appeal that touches our heart is precious, because our heavenly Father delights in caring for and comforting His children. However, if times of crisis are the only times we go to the Lord in prayer, then prayer can become a parachute that we only open when we have a need or an agenda to be served.

When there is no crisis to motivate us, and no one watching to cheer us on, we must rely on our own desire to know God and be close to Him. I call this type of prayer perspirational because it involves the daily walking out of our commitment to pray, and it is hard work. Rather than being crisis-oriented, it is Christ-oriented. It is prayer from Him, by Him, for Him, and unto Him. This type of prayer is what Paul was referring to when he said, "Pray continually" (I Thessalonians 5:17), and it flows out of a spirit that says, "Because He is worthy, I will pray." Rather than responding to a feeling or a situation, we can respond to Jesus' absolute holiness and His amazing love for us. We can depend on Him and look forward to being with Him. Perspirational prayer was the bread and butter of the disciples' prayer lives.

The idea of taking time to develop a long term prayer plan must be based on perspirational prayer if it is to last. To pray this price is to assess where we are, make a plan that is realistic and measurable, give it a time line, assign responsibility, affirm people who pray, and then celebrate the results. I know for some, this may sound too methodical to be applied to such an intimate experience as prayer, but I think in reality, planning our prayer time actually makes it more rewarding and fulfilling.

If you have read any literature at all on maintaining marriage relationships, you have probably learned that in today's fast-paced society, husbands and wives should schedule time to be together. The reason, of course, is that if we do not schedule it, it usually will not happen, and over a period of time, the relationship will suffer. While at first it may seem impersonal or insincere to "schedule" a date with your wife, I have found the opposite to be true. When my wife and I set aside a specific time to be together, if anything, I think the time is even more meaningful and intimate because we have each affirmed the other's importance in our lives.

In the same way, scheduling prayer is a way of expressing our love and gratitude to God. The more committed we are to spending time with Him, the more we affirm His importance to us. The end result is a stronger, more intimate relationship. We have no reason to feel that there is anything unspiritual about planning and working to be a house of prayer.

Joe Harding has certainly demonstrated the power of vision and planning in his Vision 2000 emphasis. More churches and conferences have been blessed by Vision 2000 than we will ever know. He basically called churches to build a vision and plan with growth in mind. Why not include prayer in such a magnanimous task—at the local church level, the district level, or in a conference?

As you assess where you are, you find out who is already praying in your church, what prayer ministries are already in place, and which ground might be fertile for planting. Every church has untapped resources that could be utilized to pray for long term goals. Every church has a junk room that could be turned into a prayer room. And every church has an energetic, spark plug of a prayer coordinator just waiting to be discovered. You probably have many people who are praying already who would light up with renewed passion if they were given some direction and appreciation.

As you begin to build your prayer ministry, take into account your current status, and make sure your plans are realistic. They should challenge you a little, but not so much that failure is inevitable. If I have learned one thing in all of my travels, it is that every church has different personalities, resources, visions, strengths and weaknesses, and all of these must be taken into account. Plans can be well thought out, bold and exciting, but if they do not match up with your church's particular giftings, they will result in unnecessary frustration and disappointment.

Several years ago, I visited a small First United Methodist Church to conduct a short workshop on the value of having a prayer room. After the workshop, that pastor and his small but dedicated congregation were so excited about the idea, they decided to open up a spare room in their building for twenty-four hour prayer. They created several prayer stations according to Dick Eastman's book *The Hour That Changes the World*, and began signing people up around the clock.

About six months later, I got a call from the pastor who was, as you might guess, frustrated and confused. "They were so excited at first," he said, "but after a month or two, interest fell off and it became a struggle. I even feel embarrassed about the fact that we failed. I don't understand what happened."

After visiting with him on the phone, I learned that the church had a strong outreach to elderly people and shut-ins in their community, so I suggested that part of the prayer room be designated to reflect the needs and victories of this particular ministry. I also learned that they had a core of very active youth who had a vision for their school, so I recommended they might hang a special board in the prayer room where kids could leave prayer requests and praise reports, and that he challenge those youth to fill up certain hours in the schedule. We also decided that since they were small in numbers, they could set as their goal 40 hours of prayer a week, signing people up from noon to 8:00 p.m. on weekdays only instead of around the clock, and reserving two hours in the afternoons for the youth.

A few months later, I called to check on how things were going, and he was a different man! The time slots were full, testimonies were beginning to come in, and his people were excited about the new prayer room. In textbook form, it had little appeal to keep housewives and business men motivated to give up an hour of their time. But when it was personalized to reflect and include those things which were important to his people, they responded with excitement and a sense of purpose. The outcome was a prayer ministry that touched the community and blessed the intercessors as well.

Setting goals that are not out of reach is important, and it is also important to set goals that are measurable. You might want to involve at least 10% of your church in some type of prayer ministry over a twelve month period. Or you might aim to have prayer advocates in place in every church in your district by the next charge conference. Setting goals like these allows you to easily evaluate how much progress you have made and when the goals have been met. As with any big task, it is a good idea to set small intermediate objectives that lead to the desired result, so that as each step is accomplished, a sense of fulfillment and success is built in. We all believe in taking financial pledges and counting money. We consider that spiritual. Why not regard prayer with the same precision and urgency?

Chapelwood United Methodist Church in Houston, Texas has a prayer ministry team lead by one of their staff members, Matt Russell, and a lay leader, Phil Grose. They set forth some specific goals and objectives for their overall prayer ministry, and they assigned each one a target completion date. Part of their plan was stated as follows:

I. To Develop a vital Prayer Ministry
    A. Define the key components of a vital prayer ministry.
        1. Evaluate vital prayer ministries of other churches.
        2. Identify and assemble the existing CUMC prayer ministries.
        3. Define the desired CUMC prayer ministries.
        4. Develop an implementation plan.
    B. Nurture and encourage a prayer life at all levels in the CUMC community of faith.
        1. Prepare a pamphlet describing CUMC prayer ministry opportunities.

> 2. Present a prayer seminar led by Dr. Terry Teykl.
> 3. Offer Faith-Alive follow-up prayer groups.
> 4. Develop and offer equipping opportunities (e.g. full quarter prayer emphasis on prayer in Sunday School)

II. To provide resources and facilities, available 24 hours a day, which support the prayer ministry.
> A. Work with Master Planning Committee
> > 1. Identify requirements of a 24 hour prayer ministry.
> > 2. Develop a resource plan to implement.

As you can see, developing a plan with specific objectives in mind gives intentionality and direction to prayer. Just like a good building program or small group ministry, prayer needs organization and accountability to be effective.

If you want to really know what is important to a person, take a look at his checkbook register and see how he spends his money. The saying is true, "Talk is cheap." It is easy to talk about the importance of prayer in our church, but are we putting our money where our mouth is, or are we putting our money where we feel the most pressure, or where it will improve our image to the public? As I visit churches and talk with pastors and leaders, I occasionally feel bold enough to ask, "How much money in your church budget is allocated for prayer?" Sadly, sometimes the look on their face is so puzzled, I just know they are thinking, "Money? For prayer? Why do you need money to pray?" In fact, in many churches, the truth is that more money is set aside for cleaning materials than for becoming a house of prayer.

To pray the price is to pay the price for a first class, organized, informed, visible, attractive prayer ministry. Good prayer materials cost money. To host a prayer seminar may require a large financial investment. Putting a line item in the budget for an annual staff prayer retreat may mean making sacrifices somewhere else. But let me assure you, it is all money well spent. When you work without prayer, you will reap the best of your efforts. But when you pray, you reap the best of God's effort. The results of prayer will move you so much further along in whatever vision God has given to you, you will not have time to do anything other than to keep praying!

To pray the price is to award and affirm those who pray. Park Place Baptist Church in Houston, Texas has an annual banquet to appreciate those who pray in their church. They have a first class meal and invite a speaker to challenge the intercessors. The Upper Room in Nashville also has an annual banquet to affirm those who give their time to that ministry. Letters, certificates, phone calls, plaques, cards, and public recognition can go a long way in letting those intercessors know the value and importance of their dedication.

As you work to initiate prayer in your church, realize that you are asking people to do something that for most Americans, is very difficult. We are not bred for prayer in this country, as some of our brothers and sisters in other cultures are. We are raised to equate independence, self-reliance, and confidence with strength, while we are taught that dependence, humility, and brokeness are signs of weakness. Because as a society we place such a high value on our own ingenuity, and we believe so strongly in our own capabilities, to ask for help from anyone, even God, is like admitting defeat. To relinquish control of a situation and admit that we can not do it ourselves seems to be in direct opposition to who we are as Americans. Our pioneering mindset drives us to push faster and work harder, anything to avoid crying out to the Father, "Help me, Lord!"

As a result, you will certainly encounter negativity, apathy, doubt, discouragement, cynicism and even ridicule—and that is just from your church body. Satan will wield his own war against any prayer initiative because he knows that prayer is what moves the hand of God. You will run into all kinds of spiritual resistance as he throws one roadblock after another in your path. People may not sign up to pray, or a prayer launch may never lift off. Church "busy-ness" might crowd prayer events right off the calendar and more traditional programs may preempt them.

Nevertheless, Jesus said, "My Father's house will be called a house of prayer" (Matthew 21:13). If you have a firm, focused prayer plan, it can and will weather all the increments. You will stay on course even in the worst of storms because your instruments will already be set. The support of church leadership will give it authority, and you will see prayer begin and steadily gain momentum. And once it starts, it is almost impossible to stop because the results will be visible and dramatic, and they will act like gasoline on a fire.

Establish Leadership for Prayer

I mention leadership because it is critical to the success of any ministry. Without it, prayer simply will not happen. Churches all over the country are discovering that just as they need someone to oversee their Sunday school curriculum, music program, outreach ministry, and fund raising campaign, they also need someone to be in charge of prayer—someone other than the pastor.

Englewood Baptist Church in Rocky Mount, North Carolina leads their association in conversions, and they attribute much of their success in that area to their multiple prayer ministries. One of the reasons their prayer ministries are thriving is because they placed a high enough emphasis on it to hire a part time staff prayer coordinator. She is the spark plug that makes the wheels turn, and there is nothing part time about the way she works. She coordinates, delegates, informs, and appreciates. She works closely with her pastor, and yet prevents him from being entangled in the day-to-day details of the ministry. And simply by hiring her and giving her an office, the pastor has made the statement, "Prayer is of fundamental importance; it is not just an elective."

Many churches, like Englewood, have realized the necessity of prayer coordinators, whether paid or volunteer. Kenwood Baptist in Cincinnati, Ohio, Frazer Memorial United Methodist in Montgomery,

Alabama, and Community of Joy Lutheran in Phoenix, Arizona have all taken that step in fostering prayer.

Another way to give leadership to prayer is to elect a prayer chairperson to your Administrative Council, Council on Ministries, or Leadership Board. This person would be responsible for gathering prayer resources, developing or initiating a prayer plan, bringing prayer leaders in your city together, and working with pastors. They might search for ways to incorporate prayer into existing programs and extend prayer beyond the church walls into the community. They could establish some kind of information network to keep all the churches in your community updated on special prayer events, and work to involve more people in prayer. A prayer chairperson, like a prayer coordinator, makes prayer visible and gives it credibility.

One of the best kept secrets of the United Methodist church is a special kind of prayer leadership group called the Prayer Advocates. Sponsored and organized by the United Methodist Men, the Prayer Advocates provide an official, "sanctioned" structure for prayer leadership within our denomination. The program was designed to place a Prayer Advocate in every United Methodist church, as well as one at the district level and one over each conference. The advocates are appointed by the President of United Methodist Men at each corresponding level—the Conference President selecting the Conference Prayer Advocate, the District President appointing at the district level, and the Men's Fellowship President appointing their own local church advocate.

In general, the role of these men is to promote prayer by supporting the Upper Room ministry and all of its facets including resources, remote prayer lines and special events. They are also to establish Covenant Prayer Groups in the local church, and work to fill all the advocate positions in their conference. According to their job description, they are to be motivated by the desire for a growing prayer life, both personally and corporately, and they are to stay informed about practical prayer materials. They are expected to attend as many special United Methodist prayer events and training sessions as possible.

Obviously, if implemented to its fullest potential, this program could be of tremendous value in calling this denomination to prayer. Unfortunately, few conferences have carried out this plan as it was intended, and many do not even know it exists. In fact, I just learned about the Prayer Advocates a couple of years ago, even though I have been pastoring and traveling in Methodist churches for nearly 30 years! They are a little known group, but one that has a heart and a vision to see prayer elevated to the same administrative level as other fundamental programs in our denomination. I become more convinced every day that the solution to the United Methodist dilemma is a spiritual one, and will come forth through prayer. It is encouraging to me to see people, especially our men, doing what they can to take the lead.

Become Familiar with Prayer Resources

Ten years after the end of World War II, it is said that an American pilot discovered an old man living on a remote island near Japan. The old Japanese soldier, still carrying his gun, had apparently been stranded there sometime during the war, and had survived for years on his own resourcefulness. Thinking the man would be ecstatic about being found, the pilot sent out a rescue team to bring him back to safety, but when they approached him, he took cover and opened fire! Because he had been isolated on the island with no radio or any other form of communication, he had not heard any news for the last ten years. As far as he knew, we were still fighting the war!

The prophet Hosea said, "My people are destroyed from lack of knowledge" (Hosea 4:6). Many pastors could probably attest to this fact if pressed about their congregations' knowledge of scripture. As Methodists we seem, in some ways, to be sadly uninformed about the new things happening in the area of prayer. I think we are similar to the old Japanese soldier who was so cut off from the rest of the world that he had no idea that life had totally passed him by. Sometimes I get the feeling that we are fighting battles that ended long ago, while exciting new developments are going on without us. The problem is, when it comes to prayer, if we are perishing for lack of knowledge, it is not because information is not available, but rather because we are simply not taking advantage of it.

In my estimation, there are at least ten major contemporary prayer movements currently operating worldwide:

- ♦Concerts of prayer
- ♦Prayer summits
- ♦Prayer rooms
- ♦Prayerwalking
- ♦Prayer and fasting
- ♦Identificational repentance
- ♦Spiritual warfare
- ♦Promise Keepers
- ♦Prayer for leaders/pastors
- ♦Houses of Prayer Everywhere

And following this surge of prayer movements is a proliferation of books that are describing what is happening. Steve Hawthorne wrote a book describing the prayerwalking movement; Elmer Towns wrote one outlining nine different types of fasts; Peter Wagner has written several on spiritual warfare; and I wrote one on how to build a prayer room, and one that will teach you how to pray for your pastor. Ten years ago, none of these books, nor hundreds others like them, even existed. This virtual explosion of prayer materials reflects a new move of the Spirit of God.

If we are to pray a new price for spiritual awakening, we must become students of prayer. We can not afford to wall ourselves in and stagnate for lack of fresh ideas, rather we must open-mindedly seek out bold, creative ways to engage in prayer for our churches, districts, conferences, and cities. Investing in a comprehensive prayer library is a tremendous step toward becoming a house of prayer. Each time I conduct a seminar, I make available a wide array of books and resources, because my desire is not just to teach a one-day event, but to inspire a hunger about prayer that will linger long after I am gone. I know that we can not implement what we do not understand, and we will never understand what we are afraid to learn about.

Recruit People to Pray

Remember the old United States Army poster of Uncle Sam: "We want YOU!"? I think the army was on to something. They knew how to recruit.

The methods you choose to entice people into prayer ministries can have a positive or a negative effect in the long haul. Unfortunately, too often I see churches using guilt, though sometimes inadvertently, to try to involve people in prayer. The problem with this is that although guilt may push some people in the door initially, they will not stay if they do not feel good about what they are doing. A better approach to recruiting is simply to let people know that prayer is *the* work of the Kingdom. You may find prayer selling itself as the Holy Spirit moves and nudges. In fact, I frequently hear pastors say that once they got a prayer ministry up and running, they actually had more people volunteering than they needed because the results were so dynamic that everyone wanted to be part of it.

For the initial stages of recruiting, here are a few suggestions:

1. Offer a variety of prayer models to appeal to different people.
2. Make everything about your prayer ministries as first class and attractive as possible.
3. Be organized.
4. State very clearly the ministry objectives and its requirements, including the date it will start and the date it will finish. This is what I call term praying.
5. Give feedback to those who pray so that they can be motivated by the answers.
6. Appreciate those who pray in visible ways.

Following suggestions like these will start your prayer efforts off on the right foot and set the stage for a positive experience for those who participate. For example, offering a wide variety of different models means that more people are likely to find some way to pray that is meaningful to them, and therefore they are more likely to feel satisfied with their involvement. Using first-class materials and being organized gives participants the sense that what they are doing is important and not just thrown together. And, giving the prayer term a definite starting date and an ending date builds in a feeling of accomplishment when the term is over. No one wants to feel like a quitter, so do not make the mistake of expecting intercessors to run a race without a finish line.

Train People to Pray Strategically

As a pastor, I know it is easy to take for granted the spirituality of your congregation. We sometimes assume that when we ask them to pray for a specific need in the body, they know what we mean. But experience has taught me that may not be the case. In fact, I believe most Christians do not really understand prayer that goes beyond a brief blessing before a meal or a quick request uttered at bedtime. For most churchgoers, the idea of praying for an entire hour is intimidating, frightening, and anything but appealing. The only thing worse would be having to pray publicly! I sometimes emphasize this point when I teach by explaining that most of my church members were so shy they would not even lead in silent prayer! Although many people earnestly want to pray, they just do not know how because they have never been taught.

As pastors, we must take at least some of the responsibility for the prayerlessness of our people. Just as our seminaries do not offer courses on prayer, most of our churches do not either. And if we are not teaching our people to pray, how and where do we expect them to learn? Prayer does not come naturally for most—even the disciples pleaded, "Lord, teach us to pray" (Luke 11:1). Many universities offer degrees in communication, suggesting that much can be learned and studied about the art of speaking and listening. Why then, do we not offer our members the same opportunities to study and learn the art of communicating with the Creator of the universe?

Let me also say that we need to be committed to training all of our people to pray, not just some select group who exhibit the gift of intercession. We can not leave the burden of prayer evangelism to those who can pray in rapid-fire mode for ten minutes without ever taking a breath. Prayer ministries will not benefit from spiritual elitism or exclusive attitudes. Jesus called all of us to be fishers of men and to bring our families and friends into saving knowledge. Men, women, youth, children—they all have a significant part to play in fulfilling the Great Commission, but we must send them out with the proper training for the job.

To pray the price means to make prayer training an integral part of church life. We must model it in the services, preach on it from the pulpit, offer classes on it for all ages, plan special seminars or workshops around it, and weave it into everything we do. And then we have to offer a wide variety of ways to practice it by scheduling prayer vigils, hosting a concert of prayer or starting new prayer groups, so that we can encourage all of our members to be involved in prayer in a way that is meaningful to them.

I feel so strongly about the importance of teaching people to pray, that over the last ten years, I have devoted hundreds of weekends, even when I was pastoring, to this very idea. Recently, I resigned my church because I felt God was calling me to speak and teach on prayer full time. Now I travel somewhere in America nearly every weekend conducting prayer seminars and workshops for pastors, individual churches, groups of churches, United Methodist districts, and even cities. We developed a 40 page teaching syllabus that contains outlines of many of the prayer models I have mentioned, and we cover as much territory as we can in about eight hours beginning Friday evening and ending Saturday afternoon. The teaching focuses on prayer evangelism, with the understanding that as we pray to win people to Jesus, we will also develop a deeper relationship with Him. And certainly mine is not only prayer ministry around; many other individuals are putting together similar events including Peter Wagner, Steve Hawthorne, and Ed Silvoso. I find that believers of all denominations, our own included, are hungry to experience more of God. Even the pastors who participate in our seminars are yearning to press deeper into the heart of the Father.

The kind of prayer I believe God is calling the Methodist church to is a "new" prayer—new in the sense that it is not interested in our agendas, but rather in Kingdom agendas. Instead of asking God to bless what we are doing, new prayer seeks to know what God is doing, and then says, "Do not leave us out!" Let us commit to learn and teach about how God is moving through prayer, so that as a denomination, we might be known above all else as a people after His heart.

Turn Plans Into Action

Visions, plans, and investments are meaningful only if they result in action. To pray the price is to do more than just talk about prayer or read about it; we must be "doers of the word" (James 1:22).

Ten years ago, had we talked about this, we would only have had a few options like starting a prayer group or forming a prayer chain. The scope of practical ideas to be implemented was limited. I remember in the early days of our church, I knew God was calling us to be a praying church, but all we knew to do was plan Saturday prayer vigils. So we did—about twice a month. We may not have been very creative, but we were committed, and it was during that time that God showed me the connection between prayer and evangelism.

I remember during one of our first vigils, my time slot was 10:00 in the morning. You must understand that being a fledgling church, our office was a very obscure store front in a small strip of businesses. Yet while I was there praying alone, a young man came to the door wanting to know if someone could talk to him about how to become a Christian. I was astounded. It was our first profession of faith, and it appropriately happened while I was praying, not preaching. I was so moved by the experience that we planned another vigil for the next Saturday, and I signed up again, this time for 4:00 in the afternoon. Again, while I was praying, I heard a knock at the door only to discover another troubled young man who was looking for answers. He, too accepted Christ, becoming our second profession of faith. For that to have happened once was almost unbelievable, but twice—I knew God was speaking to me. He showed me, "If you will find me, others will find you." Prayer evangelism works. When we pray targeting the Great Commission, people are drawn to Christ, not by our sign or our building, but by the Holy Spirit.

From then on, we built a tradition around starting a new prayer ministry each year. The good news is, as we learned more about prayer and became familiar with other praying churches, we realized we had more options than just Saturday prayer vigils. We discovered an extensive menu of prayer, with models to satisfy any taste—liberal or conservative, charismatic or traditional, small or large, new or old. And while you probably do not want to order everything on the menu at once, it is fine to sample different ideas to see which ones suit your church best. As I said before, it is important that every member of your church, if they want to, can find some prayer ministry to plug into and get excited about. To pray the price is to work at making your prayer ministry all-inclusive so that everyone can contribute.

In the back of this book, I have listed 101 different practical ideas that could be implemented in almost any church. For other creative prayer ideas, check out Bjorn Pedersen's book *Face to Face with God* and Al VanderGriend's *Praying Church Sourcebook*. Both are excellent references for any church desiring to move forward in prayer. Keep in mind, some prayer models are meant to be used only on a term basis, meaning that they are set up to run for a specified time period, while others are meant to be ongoing. A church has a limited amount of energy, time and resources, and must be realistically selective in choosing pertinent models. For example, if you decide to build a prayer room, which is definitely an ongoing ministry and would require a lot of time and expense, you may want to choose one or two short term models that are easily implemented to run while the prayer room is in progress. Perhaps the best advice is to start small and move to bigger plans as you gain momentum.

Are We "Crazy"?

Someone defined "craziness" as "doing the same things over and over and expecting different results." If we want different results from prayer, then we can not be content to just keep praying in the same way year after year. We need new people to come on board, we need new ideas and new visions for prayer. In many nations, Christians are praying the price for the unsaved in unprecedented ways. This new kind of prayer is militant, strategic, creative and persistent. To truly pray the price we must begin to treat prayer like any other priority ministry in our churches, applying the same principles of planning, recruiting, training, budgeting and assessing. We can not take the prayer life of our church for granted and just hope people are doing it, or we will find ourselves on the sidelines, watching as others carry out the work of the Lord to reach this generation.

Study Questions

1. Discuss your own theology of prayer. In other words, what do you believe about it? Do your actions reflect that theology or a different one? Why?

2. What is your church's vision statement? How many different ways can you think of that prayer might interact with that vision?

3. Discuss a training experience you have had either for a job or maybe an athletic quest. List what you consider to be the five most important reasons that you were trained for that endeavor. Can you apply these same reasons to prayer?

4. What are some obstacles to prayer in your church? How could they be overcome?

5. If you were asked to form a prayer task force in your church, who would you put on it? What do you think might be the first three objectives for prayer if you were to draw up a plan similar to the one from Chapelwood United Methodist?

3

Experiencing
God

A friend of mine sent me an interesting cassette tape while I was working on this book. It was a recording of the Friday morning session at the 1987 Congress on Evangelism taught by Dr. Vincent Synan. Dr. Synan is a professor at Regent University, and is a prominent theologian and a religious historian. Although he is now a preacher in the Pentecostal Holiness Church, he dropped more Methodist names than I even know, and he demonstrated an incredibly thorough knowledge of our history which he had studied diligently for many years in search of his own spiritual roots.

A Surprising Spiritual History

Dr. Synan's message, as he spoke to a room full of United Methodist preachers and leaders, was that every great Holiness and Pentecostal movement could be traced back to what God did in the life of John Wesley and what he taught. He said emphatically that the "greatest spiritual forces in the founding of America were the Methodist circuit riders and the camp meetings that spread scriptural holiness all over these lands as Wesley told them to." That is quite a statement. He talked of the writings of William Arthur, John Fletcher, Francis Asbury and of course John Wesley. He spoke about other churches—Nazarene, Wesleyan, Church of God, Salvation Army, Pentecostal—that were "born in the fires of Methodist revivalism."

He reminded us of our heritage of fiery camp meetings where people flocked to the altars seeking more of God, and he explained that at the turn of the century, we were the largest, fastest growing church in the world because of how God moved in those early tent revivals. Ironically, he said that people would come to criticize the Methodists for being too noisy! He went on to list fourteen spiritual contributions that we made to his own church and to the Christian faith including a basic theology and language of worship, an emphasis on holiness, an emphasis on the person and work of the Holy Spirit, and expressive praise and worship. He said that even the word "Pentecostal" first showed up in literature in the minutes from Methodist annual conferences in the latter decades of the nineteenth century, before it carried all the connotations it does today. He urged us to trace our spiritual history, not just our organizational history, to feel the heartbeat of our ancestry.

His message was a good reminder of what most of us already know and love about this denomination.

The passion and fervor of those early Methodists caused more people to be won to Christ at the turn of the century than at any other time in our history. The movement, started and fueled by John Wesley, was dynamic and life-changing, and was characterized by gatherings where people sang, danced, wept and praised so much that they were impossible to ignore! In fact, note how Charles W. Ferguson, in his book *Methodists and the Making of America*, describes what happened at the altar in early Methodist evangelistic meetings:

> All who were willing to take the first step toward the Kingdom were invited to come forward and signify their willingness to be waited upon by the workers. It was a convenient arrangement for those who were smitten but had not lost consciousness, and it did much to lend some order to the services without restraining or confusing the mourners. It helped also by encouraging prospects to take definite and purposive steps forward and toward the preacher and the altar, a place of decision.

Even the United Methodist emblem, the red flame behind the cross, that we proudly display on everything from church signs to hymnals must represent something more than organization and methodology. Have you ever really thought about the meaning behind that symbol? We were trend setters in many ways, especially in the area of prayer and ministry at the altar, and our forefathers helped to define what it means to live life in the Spirit.

Assuming the history books to be true, what happened in the development of Methodism that so distanced us from our outspoken lineage? How did we get to where we are today?

"Pneumaphobia"

I have a theory. In the 1960's a wave of spiritual renewal swept through the nation as God began to pour out His Spirit in a new way on His people. It was the beginning of what we now call the charismatic movement. New literature, new ideas, and new churches surfaced as the movement spread to all mainline denominations in some form. In our own camp, the Renewal Services Fellowship of United Methodists, headed by Ross Whetstone, was established to spearhead the ideas.

But like all new movements, it gave rise to some fanatical groups who took the new ideas and experiences to extremes and used them to confuse, frustrate, and hurt many good church folks. Charismatics all over the land pulled out and started store-front churches of their own, and the gap widened. Walls were erected. Furthermore, a barrage of fast talking television evangelists who promised miracles for money added insult to injury, and suddenly we had a new issue upon which to take sides. "Pneumaphobia", or "fear of the Spirit", set in among us and other mainline Protestants.

The problem is that we sentenced the wrong suspect. Because it was difficult to distinguish between "charisma" and hype, or maybe because we had become sophisticated and were terrified of losing our reputations, we just put stops on anything associated with the Holy Spirit—raising hands, singing choruses, showing emotion—instead of recognizing that the real culprits were those few extremists who had mishandled the gifts. We failed to take into account that any good and powerful tool can be dangerous in the hands of a poor operator, and so we threw out the baby with the bath water. The movement and everything it stood for had left a bitter taste in our mouths, and disillusioned, we sealed ourselves off from it and took our stand: No Holy Spirit antics here! We turned into "pneuma-phobiacs" who had over reacted to some "charis-maniacs."

The Church at large in the 1960's needed an awakening, so God poured out His Spirit not to start a bunch of new churches, but to set on fire the ones He already had! He sent the Spirit simply to equip us to minister to a needy world, not to divide us into factions. And yet we somehow allowed ourselves to become self-conscious, embarrassed, and afraid of the very thing we were yearning for—an intimate experience with God. For the sake of sophistication, we amputated our openness to new works of the Holy Spirit.

Not long ago, I took my three year old grandson to one of those McDonald's where they have the giant, colorful tube systems for kids to play in. I am really intrigued by these playgrounds of the nineties— I call them the "bowels of McDonald's"—and naturally my grandson loves them. But what really amuses me is watching the parents who are there trying desperately to hide the yearning on their faces to climb up in those tubes. We, of course, did not have such elaborate entertainment, and I think some of us may feel just a twinge of jealousy. Every once in a while, I actually see a dad who can take no more, and risking public embarrassment, he bolts up into the bowels mumbling something about finding a missing shoe.

Likewise, I observe many United Methodists who now seem to be looking wistfully at the way they see God moving around them. I believe some are ready to step out and embrace new ideas, but they do not want to go first and they do not want to go alone. The symptoms of pneumaphobia are wearing off, and they are simply wanting to experience more of God through the ministry of the Holy Spirit, without the extremes, and without being labeled or ostracized.

Skinny Pigs

Perhaps the opposite of pneumaphobia could be best described by a story told by my friend Dr. Mark Rutland. He tells about an evangelist who, while preaching a revival in East Texas, was invited by a farmer to see his championship pigs. When they arrived, the preacher was surprised to find that the farmer's pigs all looked skinny. He said to the farmer, "I don't know much about raising pigs, but I expected pigs of championship caliber to be a little fatter. What happened to them?" The farmer answered him, "They used to be nice and plump until several weeks ago when I came down with a bad case of laryngitis. I couldn't call them anymore, so when it was feeding time, I started knocking on the post with a hammer to get them to come eat. They caught on quickly. The only problem is, now they're chasing every woodpecker in the woods!"

Often I see individuals who have such a desire to find more of God that when it comes to spiritual experiences, they run around chasing every new fad or trend that promises excitement. They run from this church to that church, and from one revival to the next. They literally wear themselves out trying to find more meaning in their spiritual lives.

We all yearn for deeper walks with God, and for those times when we sense His manifest presence in dynamic ways. But chasing experience just for the sake of the thrill is not the answer. We do not have to live at the top of the emotional roller coaster in order to experience rich, intimate, spirit filled lives.

Bridging the Gap with a Best-Seller

I believe somewhere between pneumaphobia and chasing every woodpecker in the woods is a place where we can live and move in the power of the Holy Spirit with grace and temperance. Seeing, perhaps, the same dilemma in their own denomination, Henry Blackaby and Claude King wrote a book addressing the problem entitled *Experiencing God*. The study series (including workbook and videos) has been a best seller in the Southern Baptist Church and in many other circles as well in part, I believe, because it has done much to narrow the canyon between charismatics and mainliners. The book touches on basic Christian themes such as how to know God's will, how to hear from God, and how God speaks today.

Blackaby and King challenge the church to leave the programmatic approach behind and embrace God's agenda. In other words, instead of asking God to bless what we are doing every year, seek to find out what God is doing and blessing and go along with that. In a very powerful way, they explain the cycle of God's people being called, being blessed, becoming a great church, and then substituting other things for a radical trust in Him. Many people do experience more of God as they work through this epistle to the contemporary Church. Its overwhelming success indicates the hunger among even "non-Charismatic" Christians to enrich and deepen their spiritual lives.

Looking for More

I know that as Methodists, our people are starving for a fresh touch from God. I believe, like the Baptists, if someone could offer us a respectable way to experience the excitement and intensity for God that is so clearly reflected in our heritage, we would devour it in a heartbeat.

This need for spiritual awakening is confirmed as I travel around the country doing Schools of Prayer, speaking in many different kinds of churches. When I have the opportunity to teach in a church that is not Methodist, I sometimes ask the question, "How many of you used to be Methodist?" In every place, twenty-five to thirty percent of the people will raise their hands. I have found our missing children!

When I can, I draw one or two aside and ask them why they left, and I am amazed at the similarity of their answers. They were not displeased with doctrinal stands or with social issues or even church polity. They left for one reason—to "find more of God." I am convinced that we are losing our members primarily because we are somehow failing to meet the deepest yearning they have to experience all God has to offer them. They are leaving finely-run, well-managed churches in search of a genuine spiritual experience. They are looking, whether they know it or not, for an acceptable way to be reacquainted with the person and work of the Holy Spirit.

The challenge is still before us to answer the need. The exciting news is that if Baptists are moving into deeper walks without being labeled or losing respect, I know that Methodists can too. We can experience more of what God has to offer us through renewed prayer, true repentance, and fresh encounters with the Holy Spirit. We can wipe out pneumaphobia completely and throw out the welcome mat that reads, "Come, Holy Spirit!" He will come gently and tread softly.

The Holy Spirit and Prayer

When we pray, we receive the Holy Spirit. And when we pray, the Holy Spirit receives us. That is why prayer is so important. As a denomination, we will not have an awakening without the Holy Spirit, and therefore we must invite him back into everything we do. In my book, *Making Room to Pray*, detailing how and why to build a prayer room, I explain the relationship between prayer and the Holy Spirit in some detail, but let me summarize it here.

The relationship is illustrated in Luke 3:31 which says, "And as he was praying, heaven was opened and the Holy Spirit descended on him...." As Jesus prayed, He received the Holy Spirit. Then in the next chapter we read, "Jesus returned to Galilee in the power of the Spirit" (Luke 4:14). In Luke 4:18 Jesus said, "The Spirit of the Lord is on me, because he has anointed me to preach good news to the poor." In Luke 5:16, we read, "But Jesus often withdrew to lonely places and prayed" and in the next verse, "And the power of the Lord was present for him to heal the sick." In Luke 6:12 He spent the whole night praying. Then Luke 6:19 says, "...and the people all tried to touch him, because power was coming from him and healing them all." When Jesus prayed, He received the Spirit's power.

He summed up His teaching about the Holy Spirit with these words, "If you then, though you are evil, know how to give good gifts to your children, how much more will your Father in heaven give the Holy Spirit to those who ask him!" (Luke 11:13). Prayer is an engraved invitation for the Holy Spirit to come.

The book of Acts is a testimony to this prayer principle as seen in the lives of the disciples. In Acts 1:14 they prayed, and in Acts 2 the Holy Spirit came upon them. In Acts 4:31 they prayed, and the Evangelist came. In Acts 8:15 "they prayed for them that they might receive the Holy Spirit." The pattern is simple: they prayed, the Holy Spirit came, and they evangelized. And as you know, thousands of people were saved as a result of their preaching. For the disciples, praying was like inhaling the breath of God, and evangelism happened naturally as they exhaled what they had received.

It is this relationship that makes praying the price so important and so powerful! The more we learn to posture ourselves, praying continually in total dependence on Him, the more freedom we give the Spirit to move and work. Remember in Luke 11, God promises to send the Holy Spirit to those who ask. Obviously, this is not a one time shot of spiritual power when we are converted, but rather the result of a constant asking and seeking for Him to send His Spirit to enable and enliven us.

The Holy Spirit is the real Evangelist. We are only here to release Him to work. This is the basis of prayer evangelism—that when we pray, He works not only in us, but also in the non-believer to accomplish God's purpose.

The Holy Spirit's Work in Us

1. Compassion

"For God so loved the world He gave His only son" (John 3:16). To have a passion for evangelism is to care enough about the souls of those we meet that we will go to any length to see that they are secured for eternity. We reach out to people because we love, and we love because He first loved us. Love is the driving force. The first thing the Spirit does in us when we begin to pray is to put the compassion of Jesus in our hearts for those outside the church, especially those who are hurting, confused and unlovable.

As the disciples watched Jesus be beaten and crucified, I am sure that the unjust brutality to the one they loved did not inspire in them warm thoughts of friendship or compassion for His executioners. But think about this: days later, as they prayed in the Upper Room, something was shed abroad in their hearts that enabled and even motivated them to go out in love and share the good news of the Gospel in enemy territory. Based on their own feelings, they probably would rather have retaliated! But as God poured out His Spirit on them, His divine compassion superceded their own desires, and they responded as Christ would.

In downtown Columbia, South Carolina, there is a small Church of God with about 150 in attendance on Sunday morning. Not long ago, as they were praying for revival, a homeless man found his way to the church looking for help. Without hesitation, the pastor gave the man some food, some shoes and a place to stay for the night. He helped him contact his family, and miraculously, he even found the man a job. What was amazing, though, was that God supplied the answer to all these needs within hours, something the pastor never could have done on his own. As he sent the man on his way, the pastor told him that if he would come back the following week, and bring his friends, he would provide them all with a good meal.

To the pastor's surprise, a week later eight homeless people showed up at the church to eat. Again he fed them, and invited them back the following week. Within several weeks, that little Church of God was feeding over one hundred homeless people on Wednesday nights, and they opened a special worship service for them on Sunday morning at 8:00 a.m. When I visited there, I had the privilege of attending church with about two hundred of the friendliest, happiest street people you would ever want to meet! In fact, the attendance in that early service has exceeded that of their regular worship time.

What touched me about this story was the fact that a small church with limited resources was willing to reach out in love to a group of people who had nothing to offer in return—no suits, no ties, no tithe checks and no social graces. Many of those men and women who had been turned away by society were ushered into the Kingdom by a praying congregation equipped with the Father's compassion.

2. Urgency

The second work the Holy Spirit does in us when we pray is to fill us with urgency about seeking and saving the lost.

One day the mayor of a small community was driving through the town square area when he noticed two of his own city workers doing something rather unusual. Along one side of the main street, they were working steadily, one of the men digging a hole in the ground, and the other filling it back up. After watching them dig and fill several holes in this manner, the mayor, somewhat confused, confronted the two workers and asked for an explanation. "Well, sir," replied the first man, "we work for the city planting trees, and usually there are three of us—one to dig the hole, one to plant the tree, and one to cover it up. But the guy who plants the tree called in sick today, and," he proudly announced, "we did not want to miss a day's work!"

How easy it is to fall into the habit of conducting church business as usual—get the mail, answer the phone, conduct services, order new candles, get more mail, order new choir robes, conduct more services, and answer more calls. We can become so programmed, that like the tree planters, we totally lose sight of the meaning behind what we are doing. The result is that the charge conference at the end of each year looks just like the one before. We count the cars at the Baptist church and wonder why they have more. We pass the time, as if "doing " church is our main objective.

God have mercy on us for just going through the motions! Our mission is one of eternal consequences, and we must never lose a sense of urgency about it. As we pray, the Spirit keeps before us our true purpose. He sets our minds firmly on Kingdom agendas, and instills in us the gravity of what is at stake. Urgency is the adrenaline of those who witness.

In Acts 14:19, we read about how some Jews came from Antioch and Iconium to Lystra and stoned Paul, leaving him for dead outside the city. But we read that after the disciples had gathered around him, instead of escaping, Paul actually "got up and went back into the city." What a crazy thing to do—to go right back into the midst of the very people who tried to kill him. But Paul had an urgency about his message. He knew that the stakes were high, so for the sake of the lost he took chances, risked safety and paid every price.

News flash: our goal is not to maintain a well-run church and pay apportionments! We are here to make a difference in a dying world. Everything we do should be motivated by the desire to win this generation to Christ, and if we do not have a sense of urgency about that, then we have missed the whole meaning of the cross.

3. Vision

Finally, as we pray, the Holy Spirit gives us a vision for how to evangelize our city. He will plant a vision for prayer evangelism in anyone who will pray for the Great Commission and sit still long enough to hear His response. I meet people in every part of the country who are absolutely driven by a vision God has given them for their church or city.

Consider, for example, Larry Sargent in San Antonio. He has taken a stand for Christ in that city that makes the Alamo look like a Boy Scout camp out. And I wish you could meet Jim Dorman in Flagstaff, Arizona. He is building not only his church, but every church in town. And then there is Dave Hampson, a United Methodist pastor in Pennsylvania. He is on a track toward unity in that area and he will not be derailed. I could never keep up with Daniel Bernard in Clearwater, Florida. He has a passion for the lost that reminds me of an NFL expansion team. The apostle Paul, John Wesley, Francis Asbury—all were men of great vision and purpose.

These pastors and leaders have a vision for what God wants them to do, and it motivates them past all obstacles and setbacks. They have their eyes set on bigger things than their own salary package or a new building. They are not out to make a name for themselves, but to lift up the name of Jesus over and above their own. However, as they lift up Jesus, people are drawn to them. Every time I talk to one of them they tell me how many people they baptized the previous Sunday, or how many came forward to accept Christ, and how their church is growing. Because they are willing to pray the price, God is using them in dramatic ways.

The Holy Spirit's Work in Unbelievers

1. Convict and Convince

When we begin to ask God to give us the lost people in our cities, the Holy Spirit goes to work in every unbeliever to gently convict them of their sin and convince them of their need for God. Remember, He is the true Evangelist. When we lead someone to salvation, we are only acting as the agent, because the real work has already been done by the Spirit.

Although we can not literally see this work going on, it means the difference between success and failure in all of our evangelistic efforts. If we have prayed the price, and are listening to the Father's direction, He will send us on divine appointment to minister to one who is ready to receive. Our opportunity may come over lunch with a client, on the phone with a hurting friend, or in the check-out line at the grocery store. But when God brings together a Christian who is user-friendly and an unbeliever who has been wooed by the Holy Spirit, then evangelism happens almost effortlessly.

I believe Jesus intended evangelism to be heart-sell, not hard-sell. Many people have been hurt by Christians who tried to push them into a commitment without first praying the price, and the result is a frustrating experience for everyone involved. Not only does hard-sell evangelism usually not work, it also tends to drive an unbeliever even further away from the Kingdom.

"No one can say Jesus is Lord except by the Sprit." Jesus himself said it this way, "No one can come to me unless he is drawn by the Father" (John 6:44). The gentle prodding of the Holy Spirit is the basis of heart-sell. We must realize that unless people see their need for Christ, all the preaching in the world will not make a difference. Unless they feel a heaviness about their sin, it does no good for us to show them the cross. Unless people want to be filled with the presence of Christ, it is no use singing eighteen rounds of "Just As I Am" as they stay just as they are!

2. Tear Down Walls

In every city are unseen forces that can hinder people from receiving Christ or can cause them to resist the Gospel. The second thing the Holy Spirit begins to do when we pray is to tear down walls of resistance in the city. For example, in some cities racism and prejudice are so rampant between different people groups that none of the churches can minister effectively until that wall comes down. Another unseen force that plays havoc with evangelistic efforts is disunity among believers. How can we demonstrate the love of Jesus to the unchurched when we are too busy criticizing and competing with other believers over secondary issues of the faith? When the church of a city is divided, evangelism will run into all kinds of resistance. Sometimes there are even spiritual forces that need to be disarmed in order to see a breakthrough.

You may be aware of a specific "wall" in your own city that stands in the way of the Great Commission. Part of praying the price involves asking God to remove any negative attitudes, feelings, or ideas that may be in the way of your vision. One of the reasons that pastors' prayer summits, city-wide concerts of prayer, times of prayer and fasting and other prayer movements have impacted so many cities is that they are springboards for repentance and healing, and they often result in crumbled walls and restoration.

3. Change the Spiritual Climate

Just as every city has a physical climate that affects the temperature, rainfall, humidity, and so forth, they also have a spiritual climate that may determine the fertility for evangelism. Although this concept is difficult to describe or talk about, if you have traveled much you know that every city just feels a little different. The people are different, attitudes are unique, and priorities may vary. To some degree, that uniqueness of each place is related to spiritual background and receptivity. In other words, some places are just easier to witness in than others!

As we pray, the Holy Spirit can work in a city to change the spiritual climate. But we must be persistent. Pray over the government leaders and lawmakers in your city. Intercede for the judicial system, the police and fire departments, public school principals and gangs. Pray over a map of your city, targeting high crime areas and areas that seem overrun by sin and perversion. Watch for evidence of the Holy Spirit at work to open new doors and make new ways. Be ready for Him to show you creative ideas to reach people who you thought were unreachable. Learn to pray for the felt needs of those outside the church, and then watch as the Spirit draws them to your Sunday morning service.

4. Bring People to Jesus

Finally, as we pray the price, we will see people come to Christ and be completed in Him because the Evangelist is at work. The more we come alive in Christ, the more we can offer a life in Him to others. Jesus said, "...open your eyes and look at the fields! They are ripe for harvest" (John 4:35). The end result will be seeing people living in the fullness of Christ for the first time. Christ in us and them is the hope of glory!

Experience or Personality?

As we invite Methodists all over the country to pray for awakening, the Holy Spirit will go to work in us and around us. He will put His love in us for people who do not know him, and He will lift us out of religious routines and place in us a sense of urgency for people on the edge. Jesus came to seek and save the lost—that was his purpose. We are honored to share in that purpose by helping others know him.

Praying over a city aligns us with those who are ready to hear. Divine appointments will become the norm as the Evangelist works in unbelievers to convict and convince. Pressure tactics will give way to precious acts of love and kindness inspired by the Spirit, and we will see His Kingdom advancing in the earth.

We need not be afraid of the Holy Spirit or of welcoming Him back into our churches. He is the only one who can breathe new life into this sleeping giant. I like the way Dr. Paul Cho, in his book, *Prayer: Key to Revival*, describes his first encounter with the Holy Spirit as Evangelist:

> I tried hard to lead people to Christ, but with few results. As I was in prayer, the Lord spoke to my heart, "How many quail would Israel have caught if they had gone quail hunting in the wilderness?" I responded, "Lord, not too many." "How did the quail get caught?" the Lord continued to ask me. I then realized that God sent the wind which brought the quail. The Lord was trying to show me the difference between chasing souls without the Holy Spirit's strategy and working in cooperation with the Holy Spirit. Then the Lord said

something to me that totally changed
my life, "You must get to know and
work with the Holy Spirit!" I knew
I was born again. I knew I was filled
with the Holy Spirit. Yet, I had always thought of the Holy Spirit as
an experience and not as a personality.

Perhaps we have been so limited by our fears of
some sort of esoteric experience, that we have failed to
recognize the Holy Spirit as a personality. He is the
One who is commissioned by God to help us carry
out our purposes. He is our indispensable partner,
guide, waymaker, and teacher. We can experience more
of God to the degree that we allow the Spirit to gently
blow in and through us.

Study Questions

1. Discuss the idea of pneumaphobia. Do you see symptoms of it in your church? What about in your own spiritual life?

2. In what ways do you experience God?

3. Discuss the role of the Holy Spirit as Evangelist. How would you describe His personality?

4. What evidence have you seen of Christians chasing after an experience? What do you think are the dangers in this?

5. Considering how the Holy Spirit works when we pray, discuss the relationship between prayer and evangelism.

4

Mainlines
Coming "Online"

A new term has emerged on the American church scene which has some mainline pastors shaking in their pulpits. It is a term that has been ascribed to an era that is giving rise to a new kind of church that many feel is the answer to America's spiritual doldrums. The term is "post-denominational." The message is clear: Mainline churches are a dying breed, slowly withering away to extinction, the remains of which are feeding the rapidly growing "mega" churches called "new apostolic reformation."

These new churches are not difficult to spot. Most are enormous in size, or at least in attendance, although the building may well be an abandoned warehouse or a upscale storefront. Many have multi-million dollar budgets and pastors who are visionary and apostolic. Their worship is contemporary, with at least some charismatic flavor. It is not uncommon for them to spawn several other churches as a result of exponential growth. I might add that they also are almost always typified by a dynamic, creative, "whatever-it-takes" prayer life. It is the foundation of all that they do.

I am in no way knocking the many mega churches that have sprung up all over the country, nor the godly men and women who are being used mightily to build and feed them. In fact, I bless them, because they are offering many Christians what they are seeking—a deeper experience with God. As I mentioned earlier, I can go into any one of those Sunday morning services and find scores of our "lost" members who left in search of something more than we were giving them. These congregations are not multiplying at unbelievable rates for no reason; the Spirit is moving and touching lives there, and many of those churches are leading the way toward unity and revival in their cities.

What does this all mean for us as mainline United Methodists? If it does not shake us up a little bit, and at least cause us to do some self-appraisal, then I fear the worst is yet to come. I believe we need to ask ourselves some serious questions: Are we on life support, doing only what it takes to stay alive? Are we simply existing for the sake of our institutions and our clergy pension programs? Is the most exciting thing we accomplish all year to put new siding on the building or replace the old carpet? Do we spend more time seeking permission to minister than we do seeking Him? Are we merely lumbering along, maintaining the status quo, while being left in the dust by churches that are purpose-driven and soul-seeking?

If it were not for the experience that I am about to share with you, and the information I learned from it, I am afraid I would be hard pressed to find much evidence to refute the post-denominational theory and its proponents. I might even be right in the middle of them. However, I do not think the mainlines are dead. Sleeping—maybe; but not dead. I am not ready to write them off, and I do not believe God is either. On the contrary, I think He may be preparing all His people, mainlines included, for a great work. I am convinced of this because I have discovered one of the best kept secrets of the mainline—the Denominational Prayer Leaders' Network.

The DPLN

Every January thirty or forty men and women gather somewhere in America for several days to do nothing but talk about prayer. The meeting is not advertised, and attendance is by invitation only. Why the low profile? The people who gather are all leaders in their respective denominations in the area of prayer, and they are committed to keeping their time together free from distractions that might preempt their purpose. The group is called the DPLN, or Denominational Prayer Leaders' Network.

The mission statement of the DPLN states that their purpose is to "encourage and assist Christian denominations and fellowships of churches in mobilizing and training their congregations and members to pray for effective ministry, spiritual awakening and world evangelization, and to work cooperatively with each other toward this end." For the three days they are together, they share one by one what their denomination is doing to mobilize prayer for awakening and to fulfill the Great Commission. They display and discuss new books, training materials, brochures, posters, videos—everything imaginable that might be used to call their people to prayer. They relate testimonies, ideas, struggles and breakthroughs from churches across the country that are on the cutting edge of what God is doing today through prayer.

I do not really remember how I came to be at my first DPLN meeting, but I remember feeling a little bit like a boy who had sneaked into the locker room of his favorite NFL team. I sat among many great leaders—heroes of prayer from their respective backgrounds. What those prayer leaders shared made all my religious breakers hot! Mainline churches were coming on line with new prayer in ways I might never have expected or believed. As I listened to them present with excitement how their people are praying in bold new ways, seeing dramatic results, my mind was impregnated with the question, "What are *we* as United Methodists doing to pray the price?" At the close of the meeting, my heart was burdened with the idea that someone needed to step forth in our denomination to herald a call to united prayer. If God is on the move, I do not want the United Methodist Church to be left behind.

Reforming the Standard

A few years ago, one of the leaders in the Christian Reformed Church of North America was commissioned by his denomination to spend six months doing nothing but studying new prayer movements and creating prayer materials for their denomination. So, with the blessing and financial backing of his head-quarters, Al J. Vander Griend developed some of the most relevant, practical prayer resources available.

He started by creating a seven session video-based course called *Passion and Power in Prayer*. The course is designed to lay a foundation of personal prayer that can then be applied to building a praying church. The leader's manual and accompanying student work-book offer instruction for skill development as well as opportunities to practice what is being taught. He also wrote *Patterns for Prayer* (52 Weeks of Prayer Ideas) which is designed to help believers develop disciplined and meaningful prayer lives. It offers practical prayer focuses for each day of the year including family and friends, church, the Kingdom and the unsaved.

In addition, Mr. Vander Griend put together a gold mine of information for local churches called *The Praying Church Sourcebook*. Bound notebook-style, this valuable reference is a literal library of prayer theol-ogy and ideas. It contains detailed explanations of over thirty prayer models that can be implemented by churches of any size, and offers testimonies from oth-ers churches that are already praying and a compre-hensive list of books on prayer.

Another noteworthy movement going on in the Christian Reformed Church right now is one that has literally turned the country of India upside down. Together with John DeVries and Mission 21 India, the Christian Reformed Church Home Missions Board developed a training kit for a program called *Houses of Prayer Everywhere*, or *H.O.P.E.* The concept, which resulted in over 100,000 prayer cells and more than 3 million registered professions of faith in India, has been implemented by many Christian Reformed churches as well as other churches and parachurch organizations.

Houses of Prayer Everywhere is an evangelistic plan that targets neighborhoods and cities, planting small prayer cells in houses, businesses, dorms, and apartments. It is based on the premise that if every believer would commit to pray diligently for the salvation of those close to them—family members, friends, neighbors and co-workers—the overall impact would be tremendous. The *H.O.P.E.* kit contains seven 25 minute training sessions, as well as training manuals, devotional guides, and other helps. It offers step-by-step instructions on starting a prayer cell, as well as principles of prayer and friendship evangelism. The goal is to win neighborhoods and cities for Jesus one household at a time.

I saw the effectiveness of this ministry first hand last year when I started it in a large United Methodist church in Houston. Even though I was only able to work with the program for a short time, I saw it grow and multiply. I trained a group of leaders for several weeks on Tuesday evenings and then turned them loose to begin nurturing their own houses of prayer.

After the first few meetings in her home, one of the ladies I had trained shared with me that praying for her neighbors had caused her to see her neighborhood in a whole different light. She said that instead of resenting the teenagers who hung out on the corner, she now felt a deep burden to pray for them. Her outlook had changed from one of indifference to one of compassion. Another couple that was hosting a house of prayer told me that they were being blessed themselves because they had been looking for a ministry they could really enjoy together, and praying for their friends and neighbors had heightened their own prayer life with each other.

One of the men in our leadership group invited me to come visit their "house" of prayer which was held in his office building from noon to 1:00 p.m. on Thursdays. He worked for the local telephone company, and had invited several of his co-workers who were Christians to begin praying together for the people in their building. It was really exciting to walk into that enormous office complex on a work day knowing that each person, from the top executive to the night watchman was being prayed for. Their doors and hallways were being blessed every day. And the most exciting part was that the ones doing the praying were denominationally mixed, and they were not the least bit concerned with their doctrinal differences. They were simply praying for others to know Christ. It sounds almost Christian.

Assembling to Meet God

For some time, the Assemblies of God have recognized the need for a renewed emphasis on prayer as their top priority, and currently they are doing some dynamic things to permeate their churches with prayer. In particular, they feel God is blessing their efforts in the area of prayer and fasting, and their newly established National Prayer Center.

Thomas Trask, Assemblies' General Superintendent, has written along with David Womack a book entitled *Back to the Altar* which shares a vision for spiritual awakening through prayer and fasting. And their leaders followed rhetoric with action by setting aside Tuesdays as a day of prayer and fasting for the denomination. At their headquarters in Springfield, Missouri, they meet in prayer one hour before chapel each Tuesday to intercede for the heads of our nation, communities and churches, as well as for world evangelization. They join many Christians who are rediscovering the power of fasting and who are finding creative ways to weave it into their personal lives. Their emphasis on fasting speaks of a genuine commitment to seek God for His vision.

In addition to an emphasis on fasting, the Assemblies of God recently opened a National Prayer Center in Springfield patterned after the United Methodist Upper Room in Nashville. The center has a telephone prayer line designed to meet the needs of hurting people who do not know where else to turn for help. They advertise the line with brochures, church newsletters, bulletins and bumper stickers that read, "Hurting? Call 1-800-4-PRAYER." Currently, it operates from 7:00 a.m. to 7:00 p.m. In its first year of operation this prayer center received over 50,000 calls, and thousands of answers to prayer which have all been recorded. They have also begun to divert some of the incoming calls to satellite prayer centers which can be set up in churches across the country for several hours at a time.

Much of the literature coming from the Assemblies of God reinforces their renewed zeal for prayer. Among the resources they have found the most helpful are *The Spirit Helps Us Pray: A Biblical Theology of Prayer* by Robert L. Brandt and Zenas J. Bicket, and a book written by their Women's Ministry division leader Peggy Musgrove. The latter, entitled *Praying Always*, is used as a study guide by many Women's Bible studies and prayer groups in various churches. In addition, they developed a training video series called *Decade of Harvest Video School of Prayer* which is a tool for equipping their churches for prayer evangelism.

Thawing Out the Frozen Chosen

The Presbyterians, sometimes affectionately referred to as the "frozen chosen" because of their strict adherence to traditional protocol, are taking some bold, innovative steps in calling their body to prayer on a national level. Their Committee for Christian Education and Publications, which is officially in charge of coordinating prayer ministries, develops materials and promotes a denominational-wide *Week of Prayer* for spiritual awakening. Among the materials they created for the *Week of Prayer*, one was an informative bulletin insert which could be downloaded by local churches and adapted for use in their own Sunday service bulletin. Their Committee of Mission to the World is also involved in advancing prayer through a

Week of Prayer for World Evangelization, and special programs to cultivate prayer for each of their missionaries by name and face.

Other ways that prayer is making headlines in Presbyterian literature include an annual prayer focus in their denominational magazine *Messenger*, a regionally-targeted periodical prayer letter published by their church planting committee, monthly prayer calendars published by several of their committees and agencies, and an annotated bibliography of prayer resources that is being prepared to be sent to every church.

One of the Presbyterian leaders also reported that several new efforts were being made to mobilize the church to pray. For example, their Executive Committee has asked for a five-person staff team to develop a "church-wide approach" to prayer for renewal and to report that approach to the General Assembly. He stated that this was the first time that the Church leadership had recognized the need for a mobilization of prayer at the General Assembly level. In addition, he reported that a new call has been issued to undergird evangelism and new church development work with intentional, planned and coordinated prayer efforts. That sounds like New Testament praying! He added that since 1993, intercessors have held a prayer vigil of some kind during each General Assembly.

The Wesleyans - A "Fast" Growing Church

I was very excited about the reports that came from the Wesleyan Church of America because over the past few years they have been busy making a solid case for an idea that I have always believed in—that prayer and church growth are connected.

From 1982 through 1989, their denomination experienced a disheartening plateau in growth, with no apparent change on the horizon. But then in 1990, they began to sponsor each year an emphasis during Lent called "Forty Days of Prayer and Fasting." For the next two years, in 1991 and 1992, they planted more new churches across the country than they had in any previous year since the 1960's, and their denomination saw a net membership gain of 10%. Coincidentally, the churches that showed the most dramatic numerical growth were those who had participated in the prayer and fasting initiative.

Their Director of Evangelism and Church Growth, Marlin Mull, says:

> We attribute this breakthrough in 1989 to the beginning of a yearly emphasis during Lent called Forty Days of Prayer and Fasting. Churches involved in that program, or some modification of it, led the way in evangelism, and church growth. Last year more than 1,200 of our 1,700 churches participated. Prayer and church growth suggest Siamese twins. You can not have one without eventually having the other."

The Joyful Results of Solemn Assemblies

One of the most dynamic transformations in this denominational arena has occurred in the Southern Baptist Church. According to Henry Blackaby and Avery Willis, their camp has been radically changed through a corporate prayer model known as Solemn Assembly.

A Solemn Assembly is a called time of corporate prayer and repentance based on the Old Testament model seen primarily in II Chronicles. In essence, it is an act of humility and brokeness by a people of God, identifying with the sins of a city or nation, seeking God's mercy and forgiveness to avoid judgment, and being restored to Him. It follows the format of II Chronicles 7:14 which says, "If my people, who are called by my name will humble themselves and pray and seek my face and turn from their wicked ways, then will I hear from heaven and will forgive their sin and will heal their land." Several of Israel's leaders called the people to Solemn Assembly in the book of II Chronicles, such as Rehoboam (12:1-8), Asa (15:1-19), Jehoshaphat (20:1-19), Hezekiah (29-31) and Josiah (34). Others recorded elsewhere include Ezra (Ezra 10:7-9), Nehemiah (Nehemiah 8-9), and Joel (Joel 1-2).

When God's people succumb to pride, sin and institutionalism, He calls them to corporate repentance. The prayer of Solemn Assembly is the prayer of self-examination, confession, and forgiveness. It provides a point of entrance for God to pour out His love and power on His people, and for them to enter into His presence with renewed passion. Times of Solemn Assembly are often characterized by urgency and grief over sin which has offended God, and they sometimes involve fasting, the reading of His Word, removal of all things and practices that are displeasing to God, zealous worship, and the making of a covenant. Joel called the Israelites to Solemn Assembly by saying:

> Blow the trumpet in Zion, sanctify a fast, call a solemn assembly: Gather the people, sanctify the children, and those that suck the breasts: let the bridegroom go forth of his chamber, and the bride out of her closet. Let the priests, the ministers of the Lord, weep between the porch and the altar, and let them say, 'Spare thy people, O Lord, and give not thine heritage to reproach, that the heathen should rule over them: wherefore should they say among the people, Where is their God?' (Joel 2:15-17 KJV)

In 1994, the Southern Baptists had a three hour Solemn Assembly on Wednesday night of their annual Convention. In an unprecedented show of repentance and brokeness, the leaders of that denomination took a turn toward radical dependence on God. The event made such an impression that it catapulted Southern Baptists across the nation into a movement that has had dramatic results. Many other Solemn Assemblies have been held in local churches, districts and associations, and the people are responding with excitement for prayer and for reaching the unchurched.

As a result of this prayer emphasis, Southern Baptist leaders are encouraging the placement of prayer coordinators in every state, association, and church. The coordinator's job is to promote prayer both through new, creative channels as well as through current ministries, and to involve as many people as possible from children to adults in some kind of active prayer ministry. Their newest advance is a worldwide electronic prayer network called CompassionNet (Compuserve), which facilitates prayer for their missionaries around the world. Subscribers number in the thousands, and hundreds of calls come in each day to pray for critical needs. Imagine the difference it must make to those missionaries to know that many people are praying for them by name and for specific needs that they may have!

Several excellent materials that deal with prayer and awakening have surfaced from this denomination, such as *Fresh Encounter* and *Experiencing God* which I have mentioned before. Both of these resources have touched many individuals and study groups outside the Baptist circle.

However, with all that is happening in Southern Baptist churches right now, by far the most meaningful report is that several churches have seen incredible gains in their numbers of professions of faith. As I mentioned earlier, people coming to Christ is the truest sign of awakening and the only one that has eternal value. Any church that is not seeing regular conversions is simply treading water with regard to God's purpose.

Other Denominations Coming "Online"

So much is happening on the prayer front that I could probably devote an entire book to reporting the innumerable ideas and strategies that are being developed and piloted in churches of every kind. For example, the Church of God based in Cleveland, Tennessee has enlisted 5,000 of its retired pastors to pray for revival in their denomination. In addition, they assigned to each retired pastor one pastor in the field to call on monthly and pray with over the phone. They have also asked every one of their churches to conduct a Solemn Assembly. The Evangelical Free Church helps sponsor a National Concert of Prayer every year, the last of which was televised from the Hylton Chapel right outside of Washington D. C. It is the largest televised prayer gathering in the world, led by hundreds of speakers, attended by thousands, and viewed by millions through radio, television and cable broadcasts.

Of course, for me it is the individual testimonies of local churches being turned around and lifted up that really hits home. As I travel and talk with pastors of every creed, I hear many of the same fears and frustrations, and when I can tell them about other churches that are being transformed through the power of intentional, fervent prayer, the labels we wear bear little significance because the promise of hope means everything.

Jefferson Conservative Baptist Church in the rural town of Jefferson, Oregon is one of those rays of hope. For years, they struggled along averaging 200 in attendance. But they were part of a denomination that was getting serious about prayer. In the Conservative Baptist Church of America headquarters, leaders were launching a program called "Mission 21 Thrust," making prayer their number one priority. Their prayer coordinator, Diane Ginter, stated that the imperative was to "develop and exercise the spirit of passionate, one-minded, united prayer" so that they might be known as a "house of prayer."

Within that framework, the pastor of Jefferson Baptist, Dee Duke, attended a prayer summit, where he caught a vision of prayer evangelism and returned to begin saturating his church in prayer. Within three years, the attendance had jumped to an astounding 1,300—astounding because the town only has 900 residents! Today, they have a twenty-four hour prayer chain that intercedes over pages and pages of requests that pour into their prayer room. Three days a week, a team of men and women devote one hour at the church to pray for the church staff, leaders and special concerns in the body. They also hold regular concerts of prayer, prayer vigils for special evangelistic programs, and community-wide prayer opportunities, as well as a number of yearly prayer events including ten days of twenty-four hour prayer before Easter and seven days of Jericho praying.

Pastor Duke says, "The results in our church during these last three years have been phenomenal growth in unity, love and caring for members of the church family and beyond, concern for the other churches in the community and their congregations, many people coming to accept the Lord..., the start of many new ministries within the church and throughout the community, and a marked numerical growth of regular attendees in our church and in other churches in this area."

God Is Up to Something

I may not be a sociologist or church scholar, but I know a pattern when I see one. When such a diverse group of denominations who have no connection to each other and who do not even uphold all of the same fundamental beliefs begin hearing the same message, it must be an act of God! When I see walls coming down, bridges being built and the people of God unifying on the common ground of prayer, I sense that we are on the threshold of something far beyond what any of us could do on our own. God is up to something—something big—and I do not want the United Methodist Church to be left out.

Study Questions

1. How do you feel about the idea of "post denominationalism"?

2. In what ways do you see other churches praying?

3. Do you see any evidence of breakthroughs in unity in your city? For example, do you know if any pastors are praying together, or do you know of any cooperative efforts between churches of different denominations? If so, to what could you attribute this?

4. I have referred several times to the fact that this new kind of prayer is *creative*. Why is creativity in prayer so important?

5. Do you agree that God is "up to something"? Why?

5

New Prayer

In one of the first little rural churches I pastored, I had an older couple who lived out on some land in the most primitive two-room shanty I have ever seen in this country. The feeble structure had no electricity or plumbing of any kind and the furnishings were minimal and crude. The old wooden frame, weather beaten and decaying, offered them little protection from the elements. While paying them a visit one Sunday afternoon, I remember standing on the dirt floor and staring up at the sky through a gaping hole in the roof!

The conditions were so bad that their son decided to build them a nice brick home on their property right behind the old one, which he then planned to tear down. So, the builders came and erected a small but attractive new home with all the comforts of modern heating, cooling and clean, running water. Although it was not fancy by any stretch, sitting there next to the shack, it looked like a mansion.

However, when the day came for his parents to move, the son ran into an unexpected snag. The problem was that the couple had spent a lifetime in the run down house, probably forty or fifty years, and they were so accustomed to it, that they refused to leave. The son pleaded with them, trying to explain how much safer, happier, and more comfortable they would be in the new home, but they could not be convinced. Although they did concede to spending cold or stormy nights in the brick house, they continued to spend their days in the shanty, cooking over a fire and carrying their own water. The situation was really somewhat poignant, watching the old couple struggle to survive, simply because they could not let go of the past. It was hard to understand how anyone could choose to live in such poverty when a better way of life was theirs for the taking, just twenty yards away.

"Shanty" Praying to a New House of Prayer

How tragic it is when we become so set in our ways that we refuse to see that a better alternative is right in our back yard. I see many United Methodist churches who live like this when it comes to prayer—clinging to the familiarity of an old shack when right outside the door is a brand new house.

For years we have lived in a prayer shanty, being satisfied with asking God to improve our golf game, further our career, give us good weather for the church picnic and help our team win. Prayer has been mechanical—we say the right words and He gives us what we want. Year after year, our prayer lives have stayed the same. We have had the same people praying the same prayers with the same focus. We have been rocking along, teetering back and forth on a religious hump, but never moving in any direction. It might even be safe to say that if our prayer life were to disappear altogether, not many people would notice.

Prayer that seldom extends outside of the four walls of our church tends to become man-centered and self-serving, seeking to accomplish our will in heaven rather than His will on earth. When we get stuck in that mindset, it is easy to stagnate and lose our perspective for what is going on around us. We continue to live in poverty in spite of the new house that is just out the back door.

As I explained in the last chapter, many mainline denominations are moving their prayer lives out of the old and into the new. They are tearing down the old frameworks of self and seeing their cities as the new prayer frontier. This kind of prayer is like a fresh wind, blowing through musty churches stirring everything up. It is others-oriented, apostolic and evangelistic.

As I have listened to the leaders at the DPLN meetings, and as I have talked with pastors and other speakers and teachers who are heralding this prayer message, I have identified seven common characteristics that new prayer seems to exhibit whether in Pensacola, Florida or Missoula, Montana.

Thy Kingdom Come

New prayer is driven by the Kingdom agenda. It is not fueled by programs or man-centered plans, but by compelling questions like, "What is God's vision for our church?" "What is His will?" "What does He want us to change, drop or add?" "How can we advance His purposes?" It is about, "Thy Kingdom come, thy will be done."

Prayer is the means God has given us to apply His power and grace to situations and people around us. Therefore, under the new school of prayer, we are praying in response to who Christ is, not just in response to some crisis. Our concern is for our neighbors, co-workers, and friends. We seek God's direction and vision for new ways to lift up Jesus in our cities so that people will be drawn to Him. Churches are realizing that they can reduce crime and promote racial healing through prayer—much worthier concerns than good weather for the church picnic or money for new choir robes.

New prayer is doing whatever it takes to invite the Kingdom of God to manifest itself here on the earth. This "all out" approach to prayer is most dramatically seen in the heavy emphasis on fasting that is currently gaining momentum. Everywhere I go, pastors, men, women, even youth are combining prayer with various types of fasts as a way to humble themselves even more, that the presence of God might fall.

I mentioned earlier how they are fasting at the headquarters of the Assemblies of God and the Wesleyan denominations. Several excellent books have been written within the last few years on the subject by authors such as Bill Bright and Elmer Towns. As well, I know first hand of several pastors' groups who are fasting and praying over their cities for spiritual awakening. For example, in Houston, one hundred and forty pastors of different backgrounds just completed a forty day fast that culminated at a city-wide rally known as Prayer Mountain. In the Metroplex between Dallas and Fort Worth, one hundred and eighty pastors have covenanted together to fast and pray for their city.

It is a well known fact that pastors like to eat. So when I see hundreds of them laying aside differences and making such radical sacrifices, I know they are serious. The message here is that all over the body of Christ, people are feeling called to deliberate, even drastic measures to set the stage for the Holy Spirit to move. They are crying out to God, saying, "We will do whatever it takes to see Your Kingdom come."

The Holy Spirit Factor

Dr. Chuck Hunter once asked me a very thought provoking question, "Terry, what are you doing right now in your church that would absolutely be impossible without the power of the Holy Spirit?" What a good question! Our church may function like a fine-tuned machine: visitor letters go out every Monday, bulletins are printed every Wednesday, the lawn is mowed every Friday and the sanctuary is cleaned every Saturday. We may keep flawless financial records, have a well-rehearsed choir, and boast of an eloquent, polished preacher. But if the Holy Spirit were to evacuate our building, would anyone notice a difference? How much of what we are doing today will be recorded in eternity?

New prayer is based on the assumption that while we may be able to do some good things with money and a nice location, we can only do extraordinary, supernatural things, such as changing lives, through the power of the Holy Spirit. We all know that marketing techniques work. Advertising works. Good outreach programs and community service efforts provide much needed assistance to people who are hurting. Good children's programs will bring in young families. Exciting singles' events will attract that group. Fellowship dinners and ice cream socials—especially if it is Blue Bell—may draw in elderly folks. The truth is, I know of many well intentioned, efficient churches that grow in numbers despite the fact that they engage in very little prayer. They offer solid scriptural teaching alongside exciting, timely programs and the people respond.

But the questions are, "How much more could these churches be growing if they were praying the price? Are they seeing professions of faith, or simply professions of church membership? If they were to pour the same amount of energy into prayer that they do their other ministries, could they spark a city-wide revival?"

I think the principle that needs to be stated here is this: We can do good works with money and programs, but we can only accomplish true ministry through the Holy Spirit. I call it the "Apollos Principle," because Apollos was a preacher who, I believe, learned this lesson in Acts 18:24-28. We read:

Meanwhile a Jew named Apollos, a native of Alexandria, came to Ephesus. He was a learned man, with a thorough knowledge of the Scriptures. He had been instructed in the way of the Lord, and he spoke with great fervor and taught about Jesus accurately, though he knew only the baptism of John. He began to speak boldly in the synagogue. When Priscilla and Aquila heard him, they invited him to their home and explained to him the way of God more adequately.

Notice that Apollos knew the Word of God thoroughly and was committed to teaching "in the way of the Lord." However, because he did not know about the Holy Spirit, his teaching, though accurate, was evidently academic, lacking the real power to change lives. I believe this is what Priscilla and Aquila gently explained to him in their home.

We must decide whether we want to exist as a charitable organization that works to better the conditions of society, or an agent of the Lord, established to spread the message of the cross and win souls for Him. If we are to truly minister, then we can never take for granted the presence of the Holy Spirit. New prayer thrives on God Himself, never on programs or perfection.

Unity

New Prayer is a fulfillment of John 17:23 which says, "May they be brought to complete unity to let the world know you sent me." It is the answer to Jesus' call for total cooperation among believers.

About a year ago at a large Promise Keepers meeting, 42,000 pastors gathered in the Georgia Dome to hear Max Lucado, a well-known author and Church of Christ pastor. He used a very simple, but clever illustration to drive home a point. First, he asked the men to shout out, in unison, the church from which they came. Of course, the answer was a jumbled discord of denominational tags. Then he asked them, "Who saved you?" The one word reply shook the stadium, "Jesus!"

This move toward unity in the body of Christ is astounding. I sense that we are entering into a time when denominational labels are going to give way to the preeminence of the name of Jesus. Just imagine every Christian in your city, in every church, praying for the same things. Imagine pastors praying together, churches coming together for concerts of prayer and city-wide schools of prayer. It is happening all over the country. The spirit of parochialism is fast receding while the spirit of unity and cooperation is rising like leaven in city after city.

In El Paso, Texas, 70 churches pooled resources to purchase billboards declaring 1997 the "Year of the Bible." The signs have a telephone number for people to call if they would like a free Bible. Each one that is mailed contains a letter encouraging the recipient to attend "the church of his or her choice." In Cedar Rapids, Iowa, several of the congregations meet together on the first Saturday of each month to worship in a different church according to that style. In Modesta, California, the churches are so unified in purpose and prayer that many of them have changed their signs to read, "The Church of Modesta." Their denominational labels are merely a subscript, or have been taken off altogether. And in Colorado Springs, 140 churches have signed a "Declaration of Interdependence," stating their need for each other and their desire to work together.

Another good example of this shift toward unity is Larry Lewis. Larry is the director of the Southern Baptist Church Home Missions Board, and naturally he is salaried by that denomination. However, they have "loaned" Larry to Mission America to serve as their coordinator of "Celebrate Jesus 2,000," a program aimed at praying for and presenting the Gospel to every home in the United States before the year 2,000. You see, at the heart of new prayer is the desire to advance the Great Commission, not just our own name or theology. If any of us could win the world the Christ by ourselves, we would already have done so! New Prayer recognizes the importance of teamwork by being inclusive of the entire body of Christ. It seeks to promote Jesus over and above any denomination or doctrine.

New Material

In the area of resources, "shanty" praying was like an outpost in the wilderness—not much new ever came along. Ten years ago, about the only books you could find on prayer were the classics by E. M. Bounds or R. A. Torrey, and maybe an occasional book of sermons. However in the new house of prayer, we are finding scores of fresh, new, colorful, updated prayer materials. The new prayer movement is not only thriving on quality resources, it is producing them as well. Finally, our books related to prayer are catching up with our vast libraries of information on methodologies and organization!

The prayer market has become a little bit like Wal-Mart—if you know where to look, you can find just about anything. In fact, new books on prayer have sprung up faster than they can be counted or read. Solid, innovative materials have been developed on every topic from prayerwalking to prayer rooms, prayer summits to prayer vigils. You can find books on personal prayer, corporate prayer, prayer and fasting, prayer and worship, prayer groups, prayer retreats, prayer for pastors and prayer for children. As churches have sought creative ways to pray, they have searched high and low for good materials to feed their new ministries. And as they work through the process of mobilizing to pray, they have put together new materials for the benefit of others. Prayer ministries today need not perish for lack of knowledge!

Grass Roots

One of the most distinctive characteristics of this new prayer movement is that it is being advanced not by well known theologians or spiritual giants, but by housewives, school teachers, medical professionals, factory workers, teenagers, and retired people. It is truly the body of Christ and not just a select group of clergy or an elite cluster of intercessors that is praying a new price for spiritual awakening. It is the "ordinary" people who are doing extraordinary things by prayerwalking their neighborhoods, claiming their local high schools, marching for Jesus in their cities, and interceding for world evangelization.

Although I could tell you about many of these spark plugs, one in particular has a truly amazing story. A housewife and mother, Betty McKinney has such a vision for unity and evangelism that she is bringing together the entire state of Montana for city-wide prayer events. Last October, she helped coordinate a state wide School of Prayer in their capital city, Helena, which drew over five hundred registrants from all corners of the state. This year in May, we are scheduled for a similar School to be held in Missoula, Montana, where again, Betty has rallied pastors and churches together to invest in and commit to learning to pray a new price for that region. I have a great deal of respect for Betty because I know that even as she and her husband battle his serious illness, she forges on, heralding the message of prayer with tenacity and diligence.

I wish you could meet them as I do, all over the United States. Organizing, giving and sacrificing, they all have a burden for the lost and for prayer. If the United Methodist denomination embraces the call for spiritual awakening, I know that it will be largely due to the heart and spirit of the people in the pews. It may not rise out of an official mandate from Nashville, but may emerge from the prayers of every man, woman and child who is willing to pray a new price to see it happen.

The Apex

In the old school, prayer was often a parachute that we opened as a last resort or when our own efforts failed to produce results. But the kind of prayer that mainline denominations are engaging in now is more than just a back-up security system. It is the apex, the foundation, the beginning and the end. It determines our course and it saturates everything. It is the life-giving center of all that we are and do, because the Spirit behind this impetus is the Spirit of God, apart from whom we are nothing.

Years ago in China, all the pastors were thrown into jail and all the church buildings were destroyed or confiscated in an attempt to kill Christianity. But amazingly, the church there continued to be one of the fastest growing in the world as more people came to Christ despite the conditions. Why? The church survived, and even flourished because it was grounded firmly on prayer. The pastors and the buildings did not define the church, but rather the church existed in and consisted of the prayers of the saints.

When I heard that, I had to wonder, "What would happen to the church in America if all our pastors and buildings were suddenly taken away? Would the church survive, or would it wither away without its material, tangible anchors?" I question sometimes the importance we place on our "stuff" and on our leaders. Neither can take the place of radical dependence on God.

New prayer sets itself at the core of everything we do. I know Jesus intended for prayer to be nowhere other than in center stage all the time, in every circumstance. That is what He meant when He declared that His Father's house should be a house of prayer. He was saying, "Above all else, before all else, and through all else, pray." I have observed in churches where prayer like this has taken hold, it begins to act like an electric current that supercharges everything they do. The more prayer power they apply, the more things begin to light up, turn on, and move forward. It brings to life all kinds of exciting expressions of Jesus, and those churches take on a characteristic glow in their communities.

A Means to an End

One of the fastest ways to kill a prayer ministry is to allow it to become an end in itself. Once that happens, people will begin to lose interest and the ministry will starve for lack of commitment. That is why, when someone asks me how to keep a prayer ministry going, I always tell them, "Attach it to the Great Commission."

New prayer is not an end in itself; it is a means to accomplishing the work of God. Remember, our ultimate goal is a harvest of souls, not just well-organized prayer ministries. For example, the unprecedented prayer force that was mobilized to intercede for the millions of unsaved people living within the 10/40 Window was not just an exercise in global organization. It had a purpose, complete with specific goals and objectives. As a result, thousands of Christians all over the world prayed with passion for people they had never even seen. They received no rewards, no recognition and no letters of gratitude. They prayed because they had a common passion for the lost. Prayer that is mobilized to carry out God's purposes will be fueled by the Holy Spirit and not by the fleeting emotions and weak wills of people.

The end results of new prayer are a deeper relationship with God for those who pray, and the rule and reign of Jesus Christ in our city governments, public school systems, churches, communities, and nation. The dividends may be global or local, but the outcome is always a measurable manifestation of God's Kingdom on the earth.

New Prayer for United Methodists

As I mentioned, I have attended several Denominational Prayer Leaders' meetings over the last few years, and it is always exciting for me to hear the latest breakthroughs and the hottest ideas. But these meetings have also been a source of some uneasiness for me as well, because every year, as they work their way around the table, eventually their eyes all fall on me, and the questions are the same.

"Who are you?"

"I'm Terry Teykl."

"What denomination are you from?"

"I'm a United Methodist."

"And what are the Methodists doing in the area of prayer that is new and exciting?"

"Well, ...um...."

I may not go back to another DPLN meeting until I have an answer for that penetrating question.

Can we, as United Methodists, join in united prayer for the sake of awakening, unity and evangelism? Can we seek to do strategic things to bring new prayer to our 37,000 churches? As God is calling major denominations to pray a new price, will we join the rest in embracing the new vision, or will we continue to close our eyes and turn a deaf ear, believing for some reason that we are exempt?

I sense that our time has come. God is calling this United Methodist Church to unite in prayer. We are a divided body with many camps: the Confessing Movement, the charismatics, the liberation theologists, the feminists. However, I believe that if we will break camp and set our face to seeking His face in a new, united way, He could pour out His grace and abundant love on this imperfect denomination.

In my thirty years as a Methodist, I have seen ideas come and go. We have tried new management approaches, and we have adopted new software packages. We have rewritten the Discipline, created a new hymnal, reordered our worship services, and restructured, renamed and reorganized every committee and agency we have. Yet, we continue to lose 50,000 members a year. We struggle for theological identity and wait for the Bishops to do something, all the while complaining about our seminaries. Why not give united prayer a try? If we are to "catch the Spirit," then we must first invite Him into our presence. Let us kneel together on a new front and ask God to forgive our prayerlessness, heal our wounds, and give us what we need to affect this generation for Him.

Study Questions

1. What do you think keeps us as a church from embracing new things, especially in prayer?

2. In what ways do you notice Christians "doing whatever it takes" to pray in the presence of God? Why do you think fasting is such a powerful form of prayer?

3. Do you see the "Apollos Principle" at work anywhere in your church? What are some good things your church is doing that might be even better if bathed in prayer?

4. In your own life, is prayer the apex or a parachute?

5. Do you know of any "ordinary" people who have done extraordinary things in prayer?

6

Stages of Awakening

As God begins to stir in us the desire to pray and see awakening come to our denomination, it is only natural that we wonder how we might accomplish such a huge task, and how long it will take to see a breakthrough in our churches and cities. If we are going to embrace the challenge to pray a new price, we need to be prepared for what lies ahead so that we will not become discouraged and give up. We need a clear understanding that awakening comes as a result of a process, not an event. It will require an ongoing application of ourselves to seek God regardless of circumstances around us. Remember God promised to "bring about justice for his chosen ones who cry out to Him day and night" (Luke 18:7), not just once a month or when it fits into the church calendar.

Persistence grounded in faith is so important because as Americans we tend to be very event oriented. We may plan prayer events with eager anticipation, but if we see no immediate results, we often become discouraged and go on to another event or try something else. I do not believe awakening on a grand scale will happen as a result of one event, or even many events, and it will not come overnight. In fact, I believe we will go through five phases as we pray for awakening: nesting, arresting, cresting, harvesting and sustaining.

Nesting

Sometimes, I think God plants in the heart of a church or even a city a picture for something more from Him. Just like an angel appeared to Mary to say, "This is what God wants to do. Is it alright with you and will you believe for it?", sometimes God will reveal to us His vision for us, and then wait for our response. We can either say, "That could never happen," or "We would rather do it this way," and go on about our church business as usual, or we can accept God's plan in faith and begin praying it into being.

This phase is the hardest because we may not see any changes or signs that our prayers are doing any good. But it is also the most important because as we pray in agreement for what God is going to perform, we are preparing the way for Him to move. We have to be still—quietly, earnestly, persistently knocking at the throne room door seeking wisdom and direction, saying, "Yes, Lord, your will be done." We do not need to run here and there, planning and scheduling, because God already knows how He will accomplish His work. He simply desires our cooperation.

When a chicken lays an egg, she does not roll it down the chicken coup saying, "Look! Look! I have another egg!" She does not run around talking about it or showing it to the other chickens. She does not even busy herself with preparations for the new arrival. She simply sits on the egg. Noise and commotion are no help. She is not concerned about how long it might take. She only knows that in order for the egg to hatch, she must patiently sit and wait for the chick to develop enough to break out on his own.

So it is with anything good from God. We must take the desire for awakening and begin to pray—quietly and patiently—until we see the revival break forth. This is the time for soaking prayer, not frenzied activity.

Jesus taught his disciples how to "always pray and never give up" in Luke 18:1-8 when he told them a parable about a widow who needed justice. Day after day, she pleaded with the judge for her cause, until finally he granted her request. He said to himself:

> Even though I do not fear God or care about men, yet because this widow keeps bothering me, I will see that she gets justice, so that she won't eventually wear me out with her coming!

Then Jesus told them:

> Listen to what the unjust judge says. And will not God bring about justice

for his chosen ones, who cry out to
him day and night? Will he keep putting them off? I tell you, he will see
that they get justice, and quickly.

Behind every great move of God is a precursor
of prevailing prayer. Consider, for example, the
Moravians. They were a Christian sect that lived in
Germany in the early 1600's. For one hundred years
they prayed systematically for revival. They were tenacious, praying twenty four hours a day for God to pour
out His Spirit in the land. And I believe that the result of
their "nesting" was John Wesley and the awakening in
England that was to become the Methodist movement.
Lasting, consistent prayer yields wonderful fruit.

This the nesting phase. Just as the disciples
prayed continually in the Upper Room, waiting until
they had been clothed with power from on high, we
must pray without ceasing. Imagine the scene of many
coming to Christ in your city and brood over it in
prayer. Wait on God, believing that no matter what
you see or feel, He will bring it to pass. Envision your
church coming alive; see in the people a new zeal for
the unchurched and for prayer; know that God will
do far above what you ask or think. Choose a time
and a place and go there regularly. Be confident that it
is His will for His Kingdom to come.

Arresting

"Come near to God and He will come near to
you" (James 4:8). It sounds simple enough. As Chris-

tians isn't that our heart's desire—to be close to God? Maybe.

I would wager that many churches make it to this point in the awakening process only to turn back. The problem is that the more we allow the presence of God into our midst, the more the light of His holiness begins to illuminate the dark areas of our lives in which we really do not want God to "meddle." Our sin becomes more and more difficult to hide and justify, and we are forced to own it and deal with it. His presence may actually make us squirm as He reveals our pride, prejudice, self-righteousness, unholy attitudes, prayerlessness, lusts of the flesh, and greed. Mario Murillo is right—before we can have a spiritual awakening, we must have a rude awakening. For some reason, we all seem surprised at what really lurks behind our squeaky clean exteriors.

While killing time before her flight a lady walked down to the airport newsstand and bought some peanuts and a newspaper. She returned to her terminal and sat down at a table to read. Having barely scanned the front page, she noticed that the man sitting next to her had opened a package of peanuts, which he was obviously enjoying. He nodded his head and smiled at her as he popped another one in his mouth. "Those are *my* peanuts," she thought. "He must have picked them up while I was reading." She slid back down behind the newspaper, indignant over the man's lack of shame.

"Would you like a peanut, ma'am?" he asked, grinning.

The lady folded her paper and glared back in disbelief. Shaking her head, she snatched up her things and went to board her plane. Once settled in her seat, she determined to finish reading the news. But as she reached into her purse, she felt a small package. To her quiet embarrassment, she pulled out her own unopened bag of peanuts.

As United Methodists, as the people of God, as Christians, it is so easy for us to see how other people are wrong. Like the lady in the airport, we often do not stop to consider that we might be the problem. We tend to habitually assume someone else is at fault and we want to blame them. Even Adam, after he had sinned, said, "The woman you put here with me—she gave me some fruit from the tree" (Gen. 3:10). However, it accomplishes little for us to point our finger at the Council of Bishops, Nashville or the Conference office. We can not put all of the blame on charismatics, liberals, other denominations or seminaries.

For us, the rude awakening Mario Murillo refers to might involve acknowledging our own self-sufficiency and prayerlessness. We must be the first to see the true picture of our own faults—how we have grieved the heart of God. We are called by His name, and as His people we are most responsible in the matter of self-examination at the cross. Any divergence from this principle blinds us to our own shortcomings and lulls us into feeling comfortable with the status quo. Part of praying the price involves repenting of anything that we have substituted for a radical dependence on God. Before God can freely pour Himself out in a fresh way on our Methodist churches, some adjustments will be in order.

More than any denomination I know, the Southern Baptists have taken seriously the need for repentance by holding Solemn Assemblies. As they began to pray, they were arrested by God! Their leadership and many of their congregations have held two or three hour services strictly for confession and repentance of anything that might be displeasing to God in their own lives, their church, or their denomination. The book *Fresh Encounter*, which I have mentioned several times, lists some areas in which they have sought forgiveness as a denomination. These are just a few examples:

- mistreating a pastor
- adopting the ways of the world
- covering up sins of the past
- failing to take a strong stand on God's standards
- isolating themselves from other churches and believers
- choosing to do good things instead of the best things
- participating in a church split
- lacking faith

How precious it is, as the Southern Baptists have discovered, when we realize how we have drifted away from God's purpose, presence and ways, and can humbly return to our first love.

I am sure much could be said at this point about sins and shortcomings in our Methodist camp. I am not at all unaware of the stirring debates and emotional battles that heat up our district meetings and Annual Conferences. But I have no desire to act as the corporate conscience of our denomination, nor assess blame or assign responsibility, so I will leave conviction up to the One who is abundantly more qualified than I am. I will ask you to consider, however, the idea that perhaps all of us—conservatives, liberals, high church, low church, transforming, reconciling—could repent of some form of judgmentalism which stems from our individual self-righteousness.

As a church that espouses theological pluralism we have many camps. In one sense, our diversity is wonderful because it protects us from attitudes of religious "clonism" which would expect every believer to look, act, speak and worship in the same way. However, a major pitfall of diversity is adversity which occurs when we consider ourselves better than another person or group. This attitude works havoc in the family of God and undermines Jesus' prayer in John 17, "May they be brought to complete unity to let the world know you sent me."

Even though our camps may be miles apart on some issues, maybe we can find a common ground in prayer—prayer for unsaved loved ones, prayer for spiritual awakening, prayer for our nation and prayer for the cities and streets where we live. Instead of praying, "God, reveal your truth to that other group so that they can see how wrong they are," could we possibly fast our denominational opinions long enough to pray in agreement, "God, we *all* need you to move in us in a powerful way and cleanse us of anything that is offensive to you or that hinders your purpose for us"? Would it be possible for us to check our artillery and our pride at the door and kneel side by side, humbly before the Lord?

Understand, I am not suggesting that we abandon our convictions! I simply wonder what would happen if United Methodists of all flavors were to rally around the Word of God and our Wesleyan absolutes and cry out for revival. What if, like allies in war time, we became so passionate about fulfilling the Great Commission that we could harness all the energy we expend trying to fix each other and apply it to winning our generation to Christ? Could it be that as we go about the Father's work, He might purify us and bring us into miraculous unity in the process?

Cresting

When we prayerfully incubate the dream of an awakening and then survive God's convicting Spirit, we can enter into an exciting phase I call "cresting." After thirty years of ministry and visiting moves of God all over the world, I have concluded that the stirrings of revival first come in waves, the crests of the waves representing the visible manifestations of God's new work among His people. After He penetrates our walls, we begin to see changes.

This time of awakening is wonderful...maybe. When people start coming to Christ it is a glorious time...perhaps. Understand that as God stirs the hearts of His people, spiritual awakening may manifest itself differently in each church. Certainly, spiritual renewal plants in Christians a fresh love for God and a new desire to know Him. Within our church services, or even in our own daily time with Him, we might sense the Spirit's presence like we never have before. We might see evidence of God's sovereign power in the form of miraculous signs and wonders, and we could feel a rejuvenated burden for those in society who are poor or needy. Someone might get healed; a night club in our city known for all types of sin and perversion might shut down for no apparent reason; church attendance and giving might increase, and unfamiliar faces may begin showing up in our pews.

These signs of awakening may not be easy for some to accept, because in many cases, they will call us out of our comfort zone and into new territory. Actually, the truth is, there is absolutely nothing tidy or convenient about a real move of God. We will be expected to welcome people into our church family who do not look like us or dress like us. We might be called on to minister to someone who is homeless or dirty. Someone might bring a guitar into the service or move the organ or sing a different song. God may even violate our personal theology by making His presence known in a way we are not accustomed to or even comfortable with. Awakening will demand that we stretch our spiritual muscles and venture out in order to receive the blessings He wants to bestow on us.

Ed Silvoso, in his book *That None Should Perish*, tells the story of how the churches in Resistencia, Argentina prayed for and received an awakening. The number of Christians exploded by 400%, and every church, small or large, was suddenly inundated with new converts. What would happen if your church suddenly quadrupled in attendance? You might be forced to expand your new members class. You would need extra volunteers to fold four times as many bulletins every week. Your services might even run past 12:00 noon! You would begin to see the phrase "parking problems" in a whole new light. You would probably have to stretch your already tight budget, add folding chairs to your sanctuary, hold more services, hire more nursery workers, and buy more supplies. And that is not the worst of it.

When new Christians start flooding into your church, you will find out why they are called "babes" in Christ. "Why is the preacher wearing his bathrobe? Why don't they serve the juice in bigger cups? Why do we have to keep standing up and sitting down? Where is the bathroom? Do we get an intermission?" They will not be the familiar faces you are accustomed to, and they will not understand the protocol. They might weep during the sermon, or laugh out loud. They might be unusually vocal, or they might fall asleep. One thing is certain, you will notice the difference. And when you feel like you have lost all control, praise God! That is exactly what you prayed for.

I remember during a time of rapid growth in the church I pastored, a couple came to us seeking money for the treatment of their venereal diseases. Because we reached out to them by paying some of their medical expenses, they started coming regularly to church. Each Sunday they would sit on the front row, unmarried, unkempt, and not well attired (although our church was very casual anyway). Their children were unruly and they often disrupted my sermons by getting up and down and generally making a ruckus.

However, because the Spirit was moving among our people, they were eventually loved into the Kingdom and baptized. They allowed me to perform a spontaneous wedding ceremony during one of our Sunday morning services, and we rejoiced with them as they entered a new life together in Christ. Their children even learned church bathroom etiquette!

In short, the cresting stage of revival will certainly interrupt our business-as-usual routines. God may call us to expand our horizons, change the way we do things, and accept by faith some experiences that we can not even explain. We may not realize how set in our ways we have become until the waves of revival start rocking the boat.

Harvesting

Throughout every stage, we must never lose sight of our ultimate purpose—to bring souls into the Kingdom. We are looking for a harvest, not just a new and improved version of our United Methodist institution. We do not just want to attract more people or regain lost respect; we want to press into the heart of God and be so mightily used by Him that His Son will be glorified in our cities. Jesus said, "Open your eyes and look at the fields (the trailer parks, the apartment units, the high schools, the golf courses). They are ripe for harvest" (John 4:35).

Regardless of how awakening may look to us, this one thing can not be compromised. As God pours out His love in a new way we will respond to Him with a rekindled passion for who He is and for His work. But that is not enough. A renewed zeal for Kingdom agendas does not equal an awakening. Although it is a wonderful by-product of revival, emotion alone will never produce anything eternal. A true spiritual awakening must bear lasting fruit.

Therefore, at the core of spiritual awakening must be salvation—new converts being drawn into the saving knowledge of Jesus Christ for the first time. Spiritual awakening is about harvest, and as you look back in history at periods of awakening, you will find that not only did people enter the Kingdom, but they did so in large numbers.

We are not just praying for an "experience" that will give us butterflies or make us feel gooey on the inside. Excitement just for the sake of goosebumps is self-serving and has little more value than the thrill of bungee jumping, which may make your heart race, but really gets you nowhere. We do need a fresh love for the Father, because He will not put baby chicks under a dead hen. But the focus of our prayer must not be on what we can derive from a flurry of excitement, but rather on the lost being saved. Spiritual awakening is not for our benefit as believers; it is for the purpose of furthering the Great Commission—of advancing God's Kingdom in this generation.

In the city where I pastored, many of the churches experienced a harvest as a result of praying the price. The highlight of my week became our Monday morning preacher's meeting when we would all gather to share with each other stories of people coming to Christ the day before. We learned that we did not have to compete—there were plenty of lost people to go around! We could all rejoice in what God was doing in the city whether it was happening in our church or the one down the street. At the end of our time, we would pray for God to do the same thing the following week. Because we were keeping our eyes on the harvest, we were not tempted to major in differences and minor in the most important. We were a diverse lot, yet we discovered we had much in common. We loved Jesus, and we wanted everyone in our city to know Him.

What grieves my heart the most about the United Methodist Church is not an issue of polity or doctrine or organization. It is not even our declining membership. What grieves me most is our lack of professions of faith. In my own conference, the last year-end report I saw showed that forty percent of our churches did not see a single person commit their life to Christ over the entire twelve months! God have mercy.

Imagine what a hospital obstetrics ward would be like if no babies were ever born there. The nurses would shuffle around cleaning the equipment, hoping someday to put it to use. The sterile little cribs would be empty and formula would sit in the refrigerators until it went bad and had to be poured out. All of the tiny stocking caps and booties would be piled up on shelves with no newborn heads or feet to wear them home. The volunteers might even start arguing about the best place to store the diapers because they would have nothing better to do!

As I move in Methodist circles, I see that many of our incubators are empty, and with no babies to take care of, we have turned on each other. I meet with some groups of pastors who are discouraged, apathetic and burned out, and they do not even know why. Yet in some cases, it has been so long since they had a profession of faith in their service they have forgotten what one looks like! No wonder they are frustrated. When a church is not experiencing the thrill of new converts, its very existence becomes stale and directionless.

As a pastor, there were times when the only thing that kept me going through three-hour board meetings and devastating church crises were the faces of precious men, women, teenagers, and children that I was privileged to see come to Christ and be baptized. I kept many of their pictures in my wallet or my Bible as reminders of why we do what we do. A pastor can receive no greater blessing than to be baptized in the tears of a convert. Those are holy, life-sustaining moments.

We are hungry for a harvest and God wants his kids home. As the apostles did in the book of Acts, we can see hundreds and thousands of people added to our number if we are willing to pray the price. The harvest is what we live for, pray for and expect God for. It is the reason we exist.

Sustaining

"Pray continually" (I Thessalonians 5:17). Now there is a powerful two word verse! How often is "continually"? My thesaurus offers the synonyms steadily, habitually, constantly, regularly, frequently, incessantly, repeatedly, and my favorite—*nonstop*. That is really a serious command if you think about it. Assuming that Paul was not trying to be humorous, he was exhorting us to make prayer our very way of life, much like the disciples did, twenty four hours a day, seven days a week. But I am afraid that if Paul could be here today, he would scarcely recognize our institutions as being even remotely related to the early church of which he was part. He might scratch his head in disbelief over how much "stuff" we have and how little we pray.

When we pray the price, we will gain new ground, but we must not neglect to sustain it through prayer lest we lose all that we have been given. John Wesley said it this way, "It is better to retain than simply gain!" How true.

When the church begins to come alive with new excitement and new converts, it is easy to get so busy meeting the demands of growth that we can get sidetracked and forget what brought it about. Prayer may get pushed again to the back burner to make more time for all of the new activities. But we can not allow that to happen if we want to sustain the awakening. We must continue to pray, and even pray more fervently, so that God will continue to pour Himself out on us.

Remember, awakening is a process, not an event. A process starts and continues forward even in the face of astounding success. It has an internal energy that drives it through both obstacles and accolades. To pray the price is a magnificent, ongoing journey.

One of my favorite churches in Houston is a 10,000 member congregation on the south side of town called Windsor Village United Methodist Church. What started as an intimate group of thirteen has multiplied to a weekly attendance of 7,000 in four worship services. The pastor, Kirbyjon Caldwell, is noted as one of the most successful, young African American pastors in the country. What I admire most about that church is that in spite of their dramatic success, they continue to have a serious call to prayer every year. One year they asked their people to fast for one week, and another year one hundred of their members committed to pray and fast from 7 a.m. to 7 p.m. for forty days! They are not taking their accomplishments for granted, rather they are praying continually, and consequently God just keeps on blessing them.

The same is true of Korean churches, where many believe the prayer movement originated. As I traveled there, I observed that the more they are blessed, the more they pray. The higher God takes them, the more they are humbled and the deeper their dependence on Him grows.

As awakening happens, we must pray continually to sustain the workings of God. We must always be searching for better ways to press into the Father's heart, and we must never take for granted what He gives us. All that we do and all that we have is for His glorification. Let us pray and trust Him for the end result.

"And will not God vindicate His elect who cry out to Him day and night?" (Luke 18:7)

Study Questions

1. Have you ever been through a time of nesting in your life when you were praying diligently for God to move in a certain way, but were not seeing visible results? What kept you going?

2. Are you aware of any corporate sins in your church that need to be placed on the altar? Who gets the blame when something goes wrong in your church? What effect might prayer have on your attitude toward your pastor, your church and the denomination?

3. Do you think your church would welcome the manifestations of revival?

4. Why should we pray for spiritual awakening among United Methodists?

5. Is an awakening really a process, or does it ever reach completion? Is it possible to sustain an awakening indefinitely?

7

From Junk Room
to Prayer Room

If we are going to embark on the journey of praying to awaken this sleeping giant, I am fairly certain we need a plan. And since we know that awakening is a process, we need to establish a way to feed it, support it, organize it, and maintain it from now until the Great Commission has been fulfilled.

As we discussed in the fourth chapter, many mainline denominations are finding creative, innovative ways to pray, and it is exciting to know that there are so many prayer ideas to choose from, that each church can literally select from the menu which models will work best for them. I do not believe at all that this prayer emphasis will look the same in every congregation because they differ as much in personality, strengths, weaknesses and callings as individuals do.

But even though we may select from a whole smorgasbord, I would like to suggest that we need a way to tie it all together. Imagine United Methodist churches all over the country linked together, praying in agreement for our denomination, sharing with each other the answers as they come. Imagine United Methodist churches in the same city sharing information with each other and praying on the same page to strategically claim every street for Jesus.

Locked Up

Several years ago I visited Korea to study the church growth movement. Naturally, I visited David (Paul) Cho's Full Gospel Central Church, which is recognized as the largest church in the world. I expected to see in action the most effective church growth strategies and promotional campaigns, and I was ready to take notes.

But no sooner had we arrived, than we were led away to another location outside of Seoul called Prayer Mountain, and I began to understand that what happened on that mountain was of premier importance.

First our guide took us to the chapel which is used for several early morning prayer services every day as well as all night prayer meetings on Fridays. He told us that it is not uncommon to find all 10,000 seats occupied at 5 a.m. Then he walked us along a path where "grottos" had been cut into the side of the mountain as places for personal prayer. A "grotto" is a little cubicle about the size of a refrigerator that people reserve for hours simply to sit in and seek God. Many of them were occupied, but as I ducked into one that was open, I knew I was on sacred ground.

I was astounded to learn that there were more places like Prayer Mountain—hundreds of them—scattered all over Korea. The Methodist Church in Seoul has its own 17 million dollar prayer center that is every bit as awe inspiring as the mountain we saw. To say that prayer is a priority in those Korean churches would be a flagrant understatement.

As impressed as I was, the real impact of that trip did not strike me until I was on my way home. I had to fly into Houston and then drive about two hours to get to the town where we lived. As I was driving, I passed church after church, and for the first time in my life, I really noticed that all of them were locked up. It was a Saturday, so most of them looked desolate—no cars, no people, no activity. I thought about all that I had seen in Korea and the passion they had for prayer. I thought about how their lifestyle reflected their absolute dependence on God as their source, and I was embarrassed at my own prayerlessness and the prayerlessness of my church. I thought about Jesus' words, "My Father's house shall be a house of prayer" (Matthew 21:13), and I realized how far off the mark we were.

As soon as I got home to College Station, I drove straight to my new two million dollar church and walked inside. The building we had worked so hard for and been so proud of, on that day, seemed profoundly inadequate. I walked though every hallway and every room. We had places set aside for our staff, the brides, the youth and the children, the maintenance workers, and even for storage. But we had no place to pray. Like all the other churches I had passed, we were locked up six days a week except for an evening Bible study or special event. I repented for not setting aside a place for the most important church activity of all. With the memory of Prayer Mountain still fresh in my mind, I decided to take action.

Making Room to Pray

The following Monday morning, I called a staff meeting. I shared with my leaders what I had seen in Korea, and announced that I wanted to turn one of our "junk rooms" into a place to pray. They liked the idea for the most part, except for one man who kept asking, "But what will we do with the junk?" We voted to store it in his garage, and to go ahead with the renovation. After investing several months and $10,000, we hung a sign outside the door, "Prayer Room."

It was a very nice room, tastefully furnished with two sitting chairs, three long tables to display information, an altar, some inspiring wall hangings, and soft, indirect lighting. We put a combination lock on the outside entrance, and closed the room off from the rest of the building so that it could be accessed twenty four hours a day without security problems. We designed it with twelve prayer stations, and equipped it with pertinent information about special needs of our members, ways to pray for myself, my family and my staff, specific prayer points in our city, and things to pray about around the world. It was no mountain, but I still believed big things would happen there.

If You Build It, Will They Come?

Now that we had our prayer room, I began to wonder how my members would respond to the idea of signing up to come and pray. I shared my vision of twenty-four hour prayer with them, and asked them to commit one hour a week for three months. To my delight, the slots quickly filled up. In a short time, we had people coming around the clock. Business men came, housewives came, teenagers came, and couples came. My staff even signed up to pray!

After the first three months, we already had a list of praise reports and answered prayers, and I knew at that point we could not have closed that room down if we tried. The people who had prayed were so blessed that almost all of them signed up again, and many who had received prayer signed up also. The prayer room seemed to generate its own excitement, and because it was so meaningful to so many people, they really took ownership of it. It impacted our church in such a way that we hung a new sign on the door, "Power Plant." One woman wrote me a note to thank me for building the room. She said, "This is what the Holy of Holies must have been like!"

Since then we have put in hundreds of prayer rooms in churches of all kinds across the nation. They work because prayer works! Just as the Koreans have demonstrated the effectiveness of prayer places, many churches, including many United Methodist churches, are experiencing first hand the difference they make in the life of a congregation and in a city. They are also discovering that prayer rooms have some unique advantages for those who are really serious about prayer.

It's Time to Pray

What is on your calendar for this week? What about next week? Maybe you have a lunch appointment with a big client, or reminders about your daughter's soccer game and your son's baseball practice. Or perhaps you agreed to be at a dinner party Tuesday evening, Bible study at the church Wednesday, and a dentist appointment Friday afternoon. Of course, all of your plans are squeezed in around your full-time job and the time you spend with your family. How did people ever get along without "daytimers"?

We are a society obsessed with schedules, and for good reason. Yet when it comes to prayer, most of us just leave it up to fate. It seems to be one of those things we say we will do in our "spare time," something which we never actually have. Why not treat prayer like any other important appointment? Why not schedule it, write it down, and plan our day around it? Write it in your date book, "Meeting with God!"

One of the greatest advantages of a prayer room is that it allows us to schedule prayer, making it much more likely to happen. For example, Union Chapel United Methodist in Muncie, Indiana turned one of the rooms right off of their sanctuary into a prayer room and signed their members up to pray from 8 a.m. to 5 p.m. during the week. Because their people sign up for a specific time, those who have busy schedules put their prayer time right on their calendar so they are not likely to forget or back out. For some reason, scheduling prayer like this also puts that one-hour commitment in perspective with other obligations, making people realize that it is an achievable discipline.

Scheduled prayer is biblical. If you read in the Book of Acts, you will see that the disciples had scheduled times of prayer—9:00 a.m. in Acts 2:15, 3:00 p.m. in Acts 3, 12:00 noon in Acts 10:9, and 3:00 p.m. in Acts 10:30. As well, scheduled prayer tends to be perspirational prayer because it is based on a conscious decision to seek God at a given time each week, not on a crisis or feeling.

In Remembrance

The Psalmist says, "Who can record the deeds of God?" And I say, "Whoever writes them down."

Go into any church and ask a few questions, and you are sure to hear about the deeds of God: people who have been healed, lost ones who have come to know Christ, financial problems that were miraculously solved, specific prayers that were answered, and so on. I think it is offensive to God when we fail to remember all he has done for us, yet what a tremendous source of encouragement it can be to recall His faithfulness.

A prayer room provides an excellent place to keep a record of all the deeds of God. In our prayer room at Aldersgate United Methodist, one of my favorite prayer stations was centered around a notebook entitled "Thanksgiving," where people wrote down all

the wonderful things God had done in and through
our church. I would weep some days as I read through
the answers to prayer and the blessings He had be-
stowed on us. Each entry in that book was a testimony of His love for us and His abundant grace, and
each one gave us reason to praise Him.

Soaking Prayer

A businessman traveling away from home spotted a sign hanging in a storefront window that read,
"Shirts Dry Cleaned - $1.00." So, he returned to his
hotel, gathered up several of his dirty shirts, and headed
back to the store to have them cleaned. But when he
walked in and laid the shirts on the counter, the man
working there said, "I'm sorry, sir. We don't clean
shirts. We paint signs."

I believe if we are going to advertise prayer, we
need to do it! One of the worst things we can do as
Christians is to tell someone, "I will pray for you,"
and then neglect to follow through with that promise.

Frazier Memorial United Methodist in Montgomery, Alabama has a twenty-four hour prayer ministry including a telephone prayer line which operates
out of their prayer room. Each request that comes in
is written on a card and then placed in a file systematically. As their intercessors come, they pray over these
requests one by one, spending as much time as the Lord
leads them to spend on each, and then marking in the
file box where they leave off so that the next interces-
sor will know exactly where to start. Because they are
deliberate and very organized, they may pray through

the box many times in a week. That means that each individual request gets prayed for not just once, but again and again! That is called "soaking prayer," and if I was facing a serious medical problem, or if one my children was in trouble, I would want my concern in that prayer room. When they say, "We will pray for you," you can count on it.

Soaking prayer is persevering prayer. When Jesus said, "And will not God vindicate His elect who cry out to Him day and night?", He was equating faith with perseverance. I believe that sometimes it takes persistent, almost stubborn prayer to reach a spiritual breakthrough because even though God is eager to answer the prayers of His people, sometimes there may be factors in a situation that we simply do not see. I shudder to think of how many prayers fell just short of the mark because we gave up too soon.

Prayer places encourage soaking prayer and give credibility and accountability to the statement, "I will pray for you." They give us a vehicle to ask and keep asking, seek and keep seeking, knock and keep knocking until we see the answer.

Prayer Made Visible

Another advantage to prayer rooms is that they serve as tangible, visible reminders of our commitment to pray the price. When a church puts in a prayer place, it sends a message to members and visitors, as well as to the community around it—"We are serious about prayer, and we want to make it a priority." It is an awesome feeling to drive by a church that I know has a prayer room and see a car parked outside. I know that at that very moment, someone is inside on their knees crying out to God in behalf of those who are hurting or unchurched. Wow!

One of my favorite prayer rooms is at Sunset United Methodist Church in Pasadena, Texas. They designed theirs around a beautiful stained glass window of Jesus praying which is set above the altar in the room. As you drive by the church, you can see that radiant reminder of their desire to be a "house of prayer."

Making prayer visible makes it more likely to happen and encourages more people to participate. I believe in doing everything we can to make prayer appealing, from investing in first class prayer materials to raising up a comfortable, inviting place for our members to seek God. Prayer does not have to be mercenary in order to be spiritual.

Hearing Aids

The Psalmist writes, "Be still and know that I am God" (Psalm 46:10). I talk to so many people who really want to hear from God, yet they are so busy running from place to place that their prayers are always shot up on the run. As a result, they never really slow down long enough to listen for an answer. God loves to speak to His children when we will get to a quiet place and wait on Him, but he does want our full attention. He will wait until our hearts are still and we are ready to hear before He speaks.

One of the simplest and yet most profound things a prayer room offers is a place to be alone and still before God. It is amazing what He will communicate to us when we go into our closet and close the door on television, radio, activity, and phone calls! Leaders can receive direction, intercessors can receive insight, those who need comfort might receive scriptures of hope, and someone might even receive a vision for the church or the city. For example, in Meridian, Mississippi, I met a local district judge who goes to the prayer room at First United Methodist every morning to listen for wisdom regarding the cases he will hear that day. In Jackson, Tennessee, Northview United Methodist recently put in a prayer room, and they have been particularly blessed by the station called "Listening." They keep a notebook open at that station for people to record what they hear from God as they are praying. One of their prayer leaders allowed me to read a few of those precious entries:

- "Jesus is here to comfort, love and care for us. Praise be to God!"

- "The power of the Holy Spirit is uplifting as God's presence starts to warm my soul."

- "I felt His presence and heard him urging me to follow."

- "I felt a sense of comfort and peace."

- "He said to me, 'I am here with you, I'm holding your hand and I will lead and guide you in all my ways.'"

- "The quietness is absolutely wonderful! I can feel God's Holy presence."

- "I heard God saying that we should be careful of the words that come from our lips—they can hurt others so much. We should be building each other up in Christian love."

- "I know things do not all work out for you every single time but they will sometime in the future actually very soon for you and I will tell your friends to respect how sensitive you are. I know God is with me."

How sacred are prayers of the heart, scribbled in the handwriting of a child. As a pastor, I assure you that knowing your people are experiencing God's presence and peace will justify every penny you spend in building your prayer room.

Because they act as hearing aids, prayer rooms also tend to generate and facilitate other prayer ideas given by the Holy Spirit to effect the whole ministry of the church in the community. For instance, while praying over a picture of the local high school, someone might be inspired to organize a group of parents or a Moms in Touch group to pray for students by name. Or, someone praying over a list of city councilmen might feel led to write a personal note to each of them just to let them know they are being prayed for. First United Methodist Church in Carrolton, Texas is praying in their prayer room for a vision to reach their changing neighborhood for Jesus. The impact on a city can be tremendous when unchurched people begin to sense that Christians are praying for them instead of condemning them.

In Agreement

If you have ever sat through a heated board meeting, you may be well aware of the destructiveness of disagreement. Likewise, in the economy of God, agreement is powerful. Jesus said, "Again, I tell you that if two of you on earth agree about anything you ask for, it will be done for you by my Father in heaven. For where two or three come together in my name, there am I with them" (Matthew 18:19-20). This means that if we can come like a symphony before God, with our hearts and minds in line with His intent, He has promised to move in our behalf. If we are all on the same page, praying bold, focused prayers in agreement as the body of Christ, we will see how eager God is to respond! Our prayers of agreement say, "Thy will be done on earth as it is in heaven."

Christ United Methodist Church in Erie, Pennsylvania has a list of government leaders in their prayer room and they practice praying in agreement over the decisions and policies made by those men and women. Several prayer rooms in Fayetteville, North Carolina have city maps on their walls marked with the high crime areas of that city. As they began to pray in agreement, the incidents of violent crime in those areas dropped by an astounding fifty percent. I even know of at least two United Methodist Conference headquarters that have prayer rooms that are prayed in each day by the pastors in those conferences. They can pray in harmony about issues that affect all of their churches because they have a central location to display pertinent information.

In His Presence

Bob Tuttle likes to describe prayer in terms of pressure systems in the atmosphere. It is a fact of nature that certain weather conditions produce large pockets of high pressure areas in the atmosphere, while other conditions produce areas of low pressure. As the "highs" push their way into the "lows", we feel the effects in the form of wind—the greater the difference in pressure between the two areas, the stronger the wind.

Now the Greek word for prayer is "proseuche," which means "to prostrate ourselves or become vulnerable before God." Dr. Tuttle says that as we humble ourselves in prayer, we are creating a low pressure area, so that the high pressure of God's presence can rush in. Again, the "lower" we become, the harder the wind of His Spirit will blow.

Prayer places invite humility and promote a visible dependence on God. As they faithfully go to the prayer rooms at St. Mark's United Methodist in Los Angeles, California, at Cornerstone United Methodist in Valdosta, Georgia, and at Trinity United Methodist in Pickerington, Ohio they are saying, "Lord, it is not by our might or power or strength, but by you alone. It is you that we need!" In Methodist prayer rooms all over the country, many are already humbling themselves in repentance and inviting God to send a fresh wind over their church and our denomination. He "gives grace to the humble" (James 4:6), and pours Himself out on those who wait in brokenness.

United Methodists United in Prayer

When I think of issuing a call to prayer in this mammoth institution, I feel a little bit like a mosquito on an elephant's rump! But from one mosquito to another, I believe if we can raise up prayer places in every United Methodist church in the country, we just might be able to get this pachyderm to dance!

We may not be able to construct a prayer mountain, but we can construct a mountain of prayer—a Methodist mountain of persistent, committed, faithful, tenacious, humble prayers for a spiritual awakening in this denomination. We can clean out the junk to make room for prayer. I have a vision for this because I believe that an assessable challenge is what we need at this hour.

We need an emphasis on prayer like we have never had before. We need a method for organizing, scheduling and focusing prayer. It is time to say, "Lord, teach us to pray a new price. Make us a house of prayer, dependent on you in every way." We need our Bishops' names, seminary names, and board and agency names in every local church so that they can be soaked in prayer daily. We need a place to listen and hear the voice of God for our Church, and a place to record and remember His faithfulness. We need a place to humble ourselves and invite His presence, to agree in prayer for His will to be done in our cities.

Imagine United Methodists from California to New York, and from Texas to Maine going faithfully, night and day, asking, seeking and knocking on behalf of the lost in their neighborhoods. Every hour they would pray—liberals, conservatives, charismatics, pro-choice, pro-life, high church, low church, new Christians, old Christians, leaders, followers, youth, seniors—casting up sails to catch a fresh wind. Perhaps the precious voices of His children would move the heart of God to not only awaken the sleeping giant, but give us an unprecedented harvest of professions of faith. As the Methodists of old did, maybe we could again lead the way toward personal holiness, unity, and prayer evangelism.

Study Questions

1. How important do you think the power of agreement might be in bringing about a spiritual awakening in our denomination? How would having a prayer room in your church be a part of that?

2. If you were to tithe ten percent of your time to the Lord, how many hours a week would you owe Him? If your church put in a prayer room, would you be willing to make an appointment with God to spend just one hour each week being with Him? How would you benefit from that time?

3. Do you ever have trouble hearing God's voice? Why do you think this is so difficult? Is God hard to find?

4. Prayer rooms make prayer visible. Why is this important?

5. Does your church have a junk room that could be turned into a prayer room? What would it take to make this happen?

8

Pray Down at High Noon!

Very early in my ministry, I pastored in several small, rural towns in Texas, and much of what I know about prayer is rooted in those early experiences. One particularly valuable principle I learned about the power of agreement in prayer was taught to me through a man I will call Lyle.

Lyle was by far, the meanest, most hateful young man I had ever come across. At eighteen years old, his parents were so afraid of him they had barred the inside of their bedroom door for their own protection, since Lyle had a habit of coming home drunk in the wee hours. He ran with a group of other rowdies, none of whom could have earned awards for civility. They were a tough bunch who easily intimidated just about everyone in town, including, I think, the sheriff.

Since I was young, bold, and a little bit foolish, I was eager to leave my mark on that small town by starting a revival and getting everyone saved. I figured that if I could reach the most unreachable person, all the others would see the power of God and come like ants to a picnic. So I set my sights on Lyle, and determined to introduce him to Christ.

I began to try to share with Lyle and I prayed diligently for his salvation. However, needless to say, he was not very cooperative. He hated me and my advances, and he began to derive a lot of pleasure from doing his best to scare me and generally make my life miserable. Sometimes late at night, he would stand in our yard, drunk, and shoot his gun off into the air, yelling all kinds of threats and obscenities. Or he would drive by in his car honking the horn and shouting things I could not even put in print. But I was so resolute and so wet behind the ears, I continued to pray daily and believe that somehow, I could reach him.

One day while I was working on my car in the driveway, Lyle wandered by with a couple of his friends and started harassing me verbally. I kept my composure fairly well until he made a very distasteful comment about one of my daughters. I could not ignore that. I put my nose in his face and was about to fire back at him a few of the thoughts that had been running through my mind, when suddenly I found myself laying across the hood of my car. He had hit me so hard and so fast in the jaw that my feet actually left the ground! I just lay there, wondering if he was going to kill me. To my surprise, his two buddies jumped to my defense, positioning themselves between Lyle and I. I heard one of them saying, "Hey, man, don't hit the preacher!" It was as if Lyle had gone too far, even for them.

My wife had been praying with me for Lyle from the start, but after some time, she became really terrified, and rightly so, since we had four young children and little protection by law enforcement. Finally one night, as the two of us sat huddled behind a living room chair while he fired his gun in the front lawn, she looked at me with a mixture of fear and absolute determination and said, "Stop praying for him. Leave him alone. He is an evil man and he deserves whatever he gets!"

She was right—Lyle was crazy and there was no way to tell what he might do if he ever really got mad. Though I could not quit praying for him, I did pretty well leave him alone, and things settled down a bit. But I figured it would not hurt for me to ask other people to join me in praying, and I began to amass a force of intercession for his hell-bound soul. All over town, and everywhere I went, I asked anyone who would to pray at lunchtime every Thursday for God to touch him. I do not know how many people I actually enlisted, but I do know that every Thursday at noon the heavens were bombarded with the name of Lyle.

After several months of prayer, the phone call came. Late one night, probably after drinking heavily, Lyle tried to end his own life by rigging a 30-30 rifle to fire a bullet into his heart. But he never was a very good shot, and when the paramedics found him, he was still alive and conscious in spite of the gruesome injuries. When he reached the hospital, facing eminent death, he asked for me.

In my thirty years of ministry, I have been privileged to lead hundreds of people through the sinners' prayer as they gave their life to Christ. All of them

were special. But few of those times were more precious to me than the moment in that hospital room
when Lyle said, "I need Jesus."

Sure enough, in the weeks that followed his con-
version, several of his friends also made commitments
to Christ and began coming to church. Miraculously,
Lyle recovered from the gunshot, and was given a second chance at life, which he vowed to make the most of.

The Power of Agreement

I learned several things from that experience—
perhaps one being that the better part of valor really is
wisdom! But more significantly, I saw the power of
agreement in prayer. Matthew 18:19 says, "Again, I
tell you that if two of you on earth agree about anything you ask for, it will be done for you by my Father
in heaven." I know that as long as we understand the
meaning of "anything" in this verse, then we can bank
on Jesus' promise.

Unfortunately, sometimes we are like the
worker who was hired to build a fence. The landowner
took him to the site, provided him with the lumber
and tools for the job, and a CB radio. Then he left
him, saying, "If you need anything at all, just ask." After
a few hours, the worker started to get hungry, and re-
membering the landowner's last words, he began thinking about how nice it would be to have a big juicy steak.
So he called on the radio, and asked for one. When the
landowner said, "No," the worker replied, "But you
said I could have anything I needed." "That's right,"

the landowner answered, "anything you need *to build the fence.*"

As long as our prayers are in line with the will of God to further His purposes, then I believe He will give us what we ask for in agreement. When I speak to a group of United Methodist pastors, I sometimes tell them this verse must have been written with district preachers' meetings in mind, since getting two or more Methodists to agree about anything can be quite an accomplishment! We are an opinionated bunch. But in the economy of God, agreement yields results, and when a church or a city really takes hold of that truth, and applies it to their prayer life, miraculous things begin to happen.

The Greek root word for "agree" in that text suggests a "symphony." Our prayers of agreement are like the harmonious blend of symphonic instruments offered up in behalf of a need. I illustrated this concept one Sunday morning during church by asking our musicians, without conferring with each other, to all play at once any song that came to mind. Of course, the result was discordant, chaotic noise. But when they were in agreement about what they were playing, though their parts were different, the result was a beautiful melody. It is pleasing to God when believers pray in harmony, on the same page. Though individually our prayers for this denomination may seem small and insignificant, imagine what a magnificent symphony would be created if United Methodists of all persuasions were to pray in agreement for a spiritual awakening in our Church.

Natural Frequency

When I lived in College Station, home of Texas A&M University, one my favorite places to jog was on Kyle Field, where the Aggies play football. Probably as well known as the Aggie football team is the military style marching band that is the pride of A&M.

I watched them practice many times, and was always amazed at their precision and exactness. After they finished a drill you could see a grid of circles in the astroturf where their feet had all landed, because their steps were so carefully measured that they literally marched in each other's footprints.

One time as I was visiting with one of the drill leaders who went to my church, I commented on how impressed I was with their accuracy, and he said, "Yes, that is why when we march over a bridge, we instruct the cadets to intentionally break cadence." He explained that in physics, there is a principle known as "natural frequency" which basically says that a force on a structure that is repeated in exactly the same spot over and over, even if it is a small force, will eventually cause damage to the structure. In other words, the Aggie band could theoretically crumble a bridge just by marching on it! But the key to the force is the unity of their cadence.

Pray Down at High Noon!

Based on what I learned from Lyle and the Aggie band, God has placed it on my heart to enlist as many United Methodists as I can to unite in prayer with me at noon on Thursdays for God to awaken this sleeping giant. We can "pray down" His Spirit to refresh us and to empower us to evangelize with apostolic results. I know that the same God that responded to prayers for Lyle will respond to our prayers now, not to save the institution, but to rekindle our flame to save the lost. As I shared in the last chapter, I believe strongly in the efficacy of prayer rooms, and how they might take us to new levels of prayer in our churches. However, I know that if that vision is ever to be reached, the commitment to pray a new price must begin with individuals. It must begin with me.

Will you join me in a "pray down at high noon?" Could you spare even ten minutes each Thursday to pause and ask God's blessing upon us, maybe lifting up some specific needs? Perhaps we could orchestrate a symphony of prayer as all over country, we go in agreement before the Father. As we bow in humility, we can experience a greater ascent into the purpose and plan of God.

Although this may seem simplistic, it occurred to me as I was writing this that I would like to see the name "Methodist" come to mean prayer. So as you pray at noon, I would offer this acronym just to help prod your thoughts, that we might be in agreement before God:

M - Welcome the Holy Spirit to **MOVE** in our midst. Pray for a spirit of prayer to fall on us. Pray for God to raise up intercessors and prayer places so that we may be known as a house of prayer.

E - Thank God for **ERASING** our sins through Jesus' work on the cross. Repent of anything in our denomination that you believe grieves the heart of God.

T - Take **TIME** to be still, listening for His voice.

H - Receive His **HEALING** and restoration for those who have been hurt by the system.

O - Pray for God to **OPEN** our hearts and bring us into unity, so that we in turn may become leaders of unity in the body of Christ.

D - Ask God to **DIRECT** us in reaching the un-churched. Believe Him for vision and creativity in our evangelistic programs and outreach ministries. Claim a harvest of new professions of faith.

I - **INTERCEDE** for the Bishops, District Superintendents, pastors, and other leaders. Pray blessing and protection, wisdom and holiness over them.

S - **SEEK** God in behalf of your pastor, his or her family, and the needs of your church.

T - **THANK** God for his faithfulness to us.

A Remnant

In the Old Testament, God often honored the prayer of one or two on behalf of many. Elijah made the difference on Mount Carmel. Joshua and Caleb made a difference. Abraham's prayer for Sodom and Gomorrah was effective. The Lord answered him, "For the sake of ten, I will not destroy it."

God is seeking a core of United Methodists to pray the price for many—just a few who are fully committed to seeing the flame rekindled. Our goal is to enlist ten percent, or roughly one million people—who will join us in this unprecedented prayer effort. I believe in the power of agreement, and I believe in the power of a praying remnant. Together, we can set the stage for the Father to do a new work because one plus God always equals a majority! Second Chronicles 16:9 states, "For the eyes of the Lord range throughout the earth to strengthen those whose hearts are fully committed to him." If you will let His eyes rest on you, maybe others will follow.

The Cotton Gin

When I was a little boy living in Bay City, Texas, I would sometimes go to a cotton gin near my house to play. One day, when I was by myself, I decided to look inside. No one was in sight. As I stood watching and listening, I was awed by the size and power of the gin. I looked up—the machinery climbed all the way to the ceiling. To my right and left stretched endless rows of working metal. It was huge and noisy, bellowing and screaming as belts were turning, rollers were rolling, and cotton was flying. I wondered to myself, "Where is the switch? Who turned it on? How could it be turned off?" It seemed so formidable, yet even a little boy could have started it moving, changed its direction, or even shut it down with the push of a few buttons.

In the face of this giant United Methodist machine, never underestimate your significance. By joining with us in prayer, you can put your finger on the button and spark a far reaching change. Let us pray the price!

Study Questions

1. Have you ever experienced the power of agreement in your prayer life? How?

2. Discuss how the theory of natural frequency applies to our prayers for spiritual awakening.

3. Do you believe God will give us "anything" we ask for, as long as it is in line with His will? How do we know what His will is?

4. When Abraham interceded on behalf of Sodom and Gomorrah, God responded by telling him that He would spare the city for the sake of ten righteous people. How could this story relate to our desire to see awakening come to United Methodists?

5. Are you willing to unite in prayer with other United Methodists all over the country to awaken this giant? Can your prayers make a difference? Perhaps you could even find a partner who would make the commitment with you.

If you will commit to pray with us at noon on Thursdays for an awakening in the United Methodist Church, please write or fax us so we may register you .

Fax: 281 355-6497
Pray Down at High Noon
P.O. Box 278
Spring, TX 77383

Appendix A: Personal Prayer Helps

Preparation

1. Invite the Holy Spirit.

Admit your need for God as you begin to spend time with Him. When you humble yourself, your personal trainer, the Holy Spirit, shows up. He is your mainstay and helper in prayer (Romans 8:26). He specializes in weakness, and He is gentle and kind. Getting things is not the primary result of prayer, receiving a Person is. The Spirit comes to fill our need to experience all God has for us.

2. Take the name of Jesus.

Praying in Jesus' name means that our prayers are offered up to God in the sweet Spirit of Jesus. It means our requests are seen in light of who He is and His finished work on the cross, not who we are or our track record. Our motives are filtered and brought in line with God's heart and will. We have His promise that if we ask anything that will further the Kingdom, then it will be done for us by the Father. In other words, is my request:

... helpful and fair to all parties?
... in harmony with the life and person of Jesus Christ?
... able to draw me closer to Him?
... going to bring honor and glory to the Son?

3. Trust that God hears you.

Prayer is not based on a feeling, but rather on the knowledge that if we come and ask in faith, He hears us and we can say, "Amen." We believe, therefore we ask (Matthew 21:21). Faith is bringing our thoughts and words into alignment with what God has already said. It is an attitude of expectation and confidence.

4. Pray the Word of God.

Take your Bible with you to pray—it is the richest prayer resource you will ever find. It is creative, passionate, accurate, and applicable, and it is our prayer language. Praying scriptures means praying the answer instead of the problem. His Word...

...is the word of promise.
...generates faith.
...is His will.
...represents His power in truth over doubt and fear.
...puts us in agreement with God.
...provides direction, scope, and variety of inter cession, insights, revelation, and illustrations.

Practical Tips

1. Be simple.

As human beings, we tend to make things more complicated than necessary. Prayer is not hard; it is a conversation with someone you love. You speak and then you listen.

2. Be specific.

You do not need a lot of words, but it is important that you are as specific as you can be with God. Make a list of people you know who are not saved and pray for them by name. If you ask for money, tell Him how much; if you need a job, tell Him what kind.

3. Be spontaneous.

Having a routine time with God is important, but always be willing to stop and talk with Him if He calls you. Love relationships thrive on creativity. Take a walk with Him or go for a drive. If He wants your attention, turn off the television. Talk to Him in the check out line or on your way to work. Prayer is not an early morning reveille to duty; it is a dynamic relationship.

4. Be outspoken.

Sometimes it is helpful to pray out loud and hear positive words coming from your lips. Verbal prayer is an excellent weapon against negative thoughts. Do not be afraid to sing a praise to Him.

5. Be conversational.

God is not limited to King's English—He speaks whatever language you speak. Talk to Him as you would a close friend, and be willing to listen in that manner as well. Learn to be still with Him and hear His voice.

6. Be in place.

Find a comfortable place that you can routinely go, perhaps a favorite chair or a porch swing. You can sit, walk, stand or even lie on your face. My first prayer place was on top of a dog house in our back yard. God is comfortable anywhere.

7. Be ready to write.

Have pen and paper handy to record thoughts, ideas, scriptures, visions and answers. You may wish to simply take notes in a notebook, or you might want to be more intentional about journaling. Any log of your prayer times will serve as a valuable source for praise and thanksgiving later on.

8. Be forgiving.

Never go through your prayer time with anger, resentment or other negative feelings in your spirit. Even if you have to forgive the same offense many times, keep forgiving. Walk in the forgiveness that you received when you accepted Christ's work on the cross.

9. Be willing to change.

You have probably heard the phrase, "Prayer changes things." Be ready for it to change you. It is a crucible for personal growth and renewal. In prayer, you can leave old habits and make new decisions.

10. Begin.

Pray for five minutes today. Do not wait until next week, or until you feel like it, or until you have cleaned up your life. Just start.

Principles

1. Praise

All prayer should begin with praise. Praise brings our focus off of ourselves or our situation and points us toward God. He is worthy, and it is the proper protocol for approaching Him. We can begin our prayer time by worshipping Him for who He is, declaring His attributes of holiness, love, faithfulness, omnipotence. A good source for praise is the book of Psalms which offers 150 creative lyrics of adoration.

2. Waiting

After entering into His presence with praise, it is good to spend a few minutes just quietly waiting on God. Isaiah 40:31 states, "...but those who wait on the Lord will renew their strength," and Psalm 46:10 declares, "Be still and know that I am God." I believe that God wants to make contact with us, but we must get still, shutting out noise, telephones, television—everything that steals our attention—and wait patiently on Him. Perhaps Jesus rose early to pray because it was the best time for Him to be quiet before the Father. Dr. Jim Jackson, pastor of Chapelwood United

Methodist Church in Houston, teaches his members to get still before God by breathing in and whispering the name of Jesus, then breathing out and saying, "Lord."

3.   Petitioning

To petition God, also called supplication, is to ask Him for what we need. It is the basis for intercessory prayer, but it is also the aspect of prayer most of us overemphasize. Jesus told us to ask, and he takes pleasure in answering the needs of those who believe in Him because it brings glory to the Father. But God already knows what we need before we speak it, and He hears us the first time. So as you petition, simply present your requests to Him and then thank Him for hearing and answering. We do not need to whine or beg. Another principle to keep in mind as you petition is that of sowing and reaping. Jesus said, "...pray for each other so that you may be healed" (James 5:16), which means to me that if you have a need, pray for that same need in someone else's life, that you may receive it.

4. Thanksgiving

Giving thanks to God is one of the main reasons we pray, because He is so good to us. His very nature encompasses all that is gentle, loving, protecting and giving. He is the same yesterday, today, and forever, and His thoughts toward you are always for your good. We can thank Him for what He did for us through His son. We can be grateful for the many ways He has blessed our lives. We can appreciate His provision, protection, and loving guidance. And we can be especially grateful for answered prayers.

5. Appropriation

Appropriation is learning how to receive from God. The writer of Hebrews says that "...anyone who comes to him must believe that he exists and that he rewards those who earnestly seek him" (Hebrews 11:6). Therefore, when we come to him it is important that we thank Him in advance for hearing our prayers before we see, feel, taste or touch the answer. As soon as Jesus arrived at Lazarus' tomb, even before He called him out of the grave, He said, "Father I thank you that you have heard me. I knew that you always hear me" (John 11:41-42).

6. Action

After our prayer time, it is appropriate to ask the Lord, "What action can I take as a result of this time with You; what can I do to bring about the answer to my own prayers?" Sometimes the Lord will give us a "holy hunch" about a specific action we can take that could result in the need being filled. We may need to forgive someone who has hurt us, dispose of something that stands between us and God, or possibly give of our own time or money toward a special need. In taking action toward the answer of our prayers, we do it in His strength (Philippians 4:13).

Appendix B: 101 Creative Prayer Ideas

1. Make a list of your blessings and simply thank the Lord.
2. Specifically ask the Lord to give you a regular prayer time. Start with a realistic goal.
3. Go to a hospital waiting room or a park bench and pray for the people you see there.
4. Put the names of your Bishop and District Superintendent in your Sunday morning worship bulletin for people to lift up in prayer.
5. Arrive early to pray for worship services. Use Terry Teykl's "Pre-Prayer for Worship" guide.
6. Start a notebook with written reflections of your prayer moments.
7. Choose a prayer model you find helpful such as the one in Dick Eastman's book *The Hour That Changes the World.*

8. Ask a prayer partner to pray with you fifteen minutes a week. Refer to John Maxwell's *Partners in Prayer*.
9. Read a daily devotional guide such as *The Upper Room* or Oswald Chambers' *My Utmost For His Highest*.
10. Go for a prayer walk in your neighborhood. Read *Prayerwalking* by Steve Hawthorne.
11. Write down prayer requests and keep a record of answers.
12. Put the names of church leaders in a prayer room or some other place where they can be prayed for.
13. Choose two government leaders each month to be prayed for in a Sunday school class or worship. Send them a letter to bless them and let them know someone is praying.
14. Find a special prayer place for your time with God.
15. Enlist people to pray for your pastor. *Read Preyed On or Prayed For* by Terry Teykl and start a class to train people for this ministry using the accompanying workbook.
16. Take prayer requests during worship services using a card that could be placed in the offering plate. Put the cards in the prayer room or give them to intercessors.
17. Initiate a series of short term fasts in your church focused on specific needs. Allow people to choose the terms of their fast.
18. Sponsor a prayer group to pray for one youth by name every day.
19. Print book markers with denominational leaders' names and place in pew caddies.

20. Read Evelyn Christensen's book *A Time to Pray* and then establish prayer triplets to pray for unsaved loved ones. You might find the "Most Wanted Card" by Terry Teykl a helpful guide for prayer.
21. Preach or teach a series on prayer.
22. Form a prayer committee task force to develop a master plan for prayer in your church.
23. Have periodic "Prayer Commitment Sundays" and give people several choices for how they can be involved in a prayer ministry. A commitment card in the bulletin works well.
24. Identify a prayer bulletin board for announcing prayer requests, answers, information and events.
25. Start a prayer library by collecting some of the hundreds of books that have been written on prayer in the last ten years.
26. Promote a prayer retreat for leaders.
27. Form a Sunday school class to study prayer. Use *Workbook of Living Prayer*, Maxie Dunham or *Blueprint for the House of Prayer*, Terry Teykl.
28. Receive a special offering for new prayer materials. Perhaps you could even sow money or materials to another church.
29. Open the church building for prayer each weekday morning at 6:00 a.m. A different leader would cover each day of the week.
30. For one month, turn Sunday evening services into well-orchestrated concerts of prayer based on the book by David Bryant called *Concerts of Prayer*.
31. Start a men's prayer group.
32. Start a women's prayer group.

33. Start a youth prayer group.
34. Invite pastors in your city to begin praying together. Read *Reunitus* by Joe Aldrich.
35. Establish a prayer room in your church using the book *Making Room to Pray* by Terry Teykl.
36. Order a *Pray the Price Kit* from Prayer Point Press. Send a prayer note to people to encourage them as you pray for them.
37. Organize a ministry to a neighborhood with door hangers from the *Pray the Price Kit*.
38. Build a prayer wall around your city using the *Watch-man Prayer Ministry* training material produced by the Southern Baptist Church.
39. Raise up some houses of prayer by using the *Houses Of Prayer Everywhere (H.O.P.E.)* training kit by Al Vander Griend.
40. Organize a group of full-time moms to pray systematically for the schools in your area. *Moms in Touch* is an excellent resource.
41. Create a wall in your church to display pictures, maps, scriptures and names to serve as prompts for specific prayer.
42. March in a *March for Jesus* in May.
43. Conduct a Solemn Assembly to repent of racial sins and other exclusive attitudes. Read about other corporate prayer efforts in *Blueprint for the House of prayer* by Terry Teykl.
44. Plan an all night prayer vigil based on the guidelines in the *Pray the Price Kit* .
45. Using a door hanger in the *Pray the Price Kit,* mobilize your church to hang a blessing on every home in your city.

46. Ask laypersons to pray with and for the pastor before services.
47. Open your church to the "Walk to Emmaus" ministry.
48. Publish a prayer newsletter. Start by establishing a special section in the church newsletter for prayer related news and information.
49. Open your altar for prayer and personal ministry during the services using prayer teams. We are currently developing on an altar training course.
50. Visit a scenic overlook with a prayer team and pray spontaneously.
51. Construct a prayer garden or an area on the church grounds with prayer points for contemplative prayer.
52. Conduct an *Acts 29 Prayer Encounter*. Renewal Ministries will help you schedule a seminar leader that will come to your church, city or district.
53. Set up a voice mail with its own phone number to receive prayer requests in your church.
54. Establish a live prayer line for people who want prayer over the phone. Publish it throughout your city.
55. Use an automated phone system to inform church members of emergency prayer requests.
56. Encourage and model prayer for missionary and global concerns.
57. Make a prayer calendar.
58. Take up business cards of your church members and put them in a place to be prayed over for twelve weeks. At the same time, enlist people to pray for your church budget using Terry Teykl's "Financial Prayer Guide."

59. Initiate a prayer chain.
60. Promote the National Day of Prayer in your city on the first Thursday of May.
61. Create a list of every member's name and reproduce it seven times. Label each list Monday, Tuesday, Wednesday.... Each Sunday, ask for volunteers who will take one of the lists and pray over each name on the specified day for that week.
62. Create a similar system to pray for visitors.
63. Discover the value of periodic prayer vigils. They can be held on a Saturday, an evening, or even for a given twenty four hour period.
64. Start prayer covenant groups.
65. Organize a team of intercessors who will pray for the pastor as he or she preaches.
66. Sponsor a local church prayer seminar.
67. Call for special Christ-centered prayer during Lent. You can use the "Christ-Centered Prayer Guide" by Terry Teykl.
68. Start a study group to go through the book *Experiencing God* by Henry Blackaby and Claude King.
69. Set up a display in the foyer of your church for Upper Room prayer materials.
70. Find creative ways to advertise and rejoice over answers to prayer.
71. Organize an Adopt-A-Cop program to pray for policemen by name.
72. Organize an Adopt-A-Fireman program.
73. Organize a similar program for city leaders and government officials.
74. Create a map of your city with helpful prayer information and distribute copies to all local churches.

75. Allow brief testimonials (30 seconds) to answered prayer during services and other gatherings.
76. Send your pastor to a prayer event or a retreat for personal renewal.
77. Host a district wide prayer event and bring in a quality speaker.
78. Pray through the book of Acts for fifty days using Terry Teykl's *Acts Twenty-Nine* books.
79. Publicize the Upper Room Living Prayer Center number (800) 251-2468 .
80. Conduct a remote satellite prayer center through the Upper Room.
81. Make use of prayer bulletin inserts published by Church Development Resources or make your own.
82. Schedule the video teaching series, *School of Prayer*, by Dick Eastman.
83. Schedule the video teaching series, *Passion and Power in Prayer*, by Al Vander Griend.
84. Initiate a church wide focus on praying for the un-churched for ninety days. You may use the "Most Wanted" prayer card or make your own guide.
85. Read *Patterns of Prayer* by Al Vander Griend to learn about fifty-two weeks of prayer ideas.
86. Read Dr. Arthur Hunt's book *Praying with the One You Love* with your spouse.
87. Pray before and during board meetings.
88. Make prayer a theme for Vacation Bible School.
89. Acquire names of people who are living in nursing homes or serving jail sentences and who would like to be prayed for. Maybe send regular notes of encouragement.

90. Develop a systematic plan of "drive-by praying" in rough areas of town.
91. Take a team on a prayer outreach. Choose an area to be prayed for and culminate with a picnic lunch or cook out.
92. Have different staff people lead prayer during the services on a rotation basis.
93. Choose a different nation each month to be the focus of special prayer. Display that nation's flag for the month in the sanctuary, and inform your people how to pray for them.
94. Purchase the *Praying Church Sourcebook* by Al Vander Griend for your church.
95. Put an altar in your home for family devotions.
96. Start a prayer team ministry for the sick. They could make hospital calls and house visits to help shoulder some of the responsibility of this important outreach.
97. Organize a prayer partner ministry for public school teachers who wish to be prayed for.
98. Put on a concert of prayer in a local civic center or high school auditorium to rally the churches in town.
99. Find out all the names of a family on your street that does not attend church. Lead your family in praying for them each week, perhaps at mealtime.
100. Break out into small prayer groups during the service on Sunday morning for a leader directed prayer time.
101. **"Pray Down at High Noon!" Pray at 12:00 noon on Thursdays for spiritual awakening in the United Methodist denomination.**

Acknowledgments

Thank you, Dr. and Mrs. Peter Wagner. You are for many of us, a father and mother in this great prayer surge. None of us will know until we get to heaven the magnanimous contributions you have both made into so many lives.

Elaine Krol, I could not begin to imagine in how many ways I have been spared, thanks to your faithful prayers.

Thank you, Francis Frangipane, for believing in me and praying for me. I appreciate your wise counsel and I treasure your friendship.

To Kirbyjon Caldwell, pastor of Windsor Village UMC, thanks for encouraging me to do this project.

Thank you, Kay, for being my wife. I value your input, your steady support, and especially your red pen! I admire and love you.

Pastor Jim and Susan Jackson, Chapelwood UMC, thanks for being an oasis of encouragement and for the title of the book.

To John Linville and Cheri Toledo, thank you for making sure every "i" was dotted and every "t" was crossed.

About *Prayer Point Press*

Prayer Point Press is an independent publishing company that works in conjunction with Renewal Ministries. It has three objectives:

1. To publish written materials for Renewal Ministries and Dr. Terry Teykl promoting prayer.

2. To offer, through event displays and catalogs, a comprehensive selection of recommended books and materials on prayer.

3. To act as a publishing service for other pastors, ministries or individuals who are seeking help with publication of quality works.

For more information about Prayer Point Press, contact:

Lynn Ponder
Executive Editor
44 Fallshire
The Woodlands, TX 77381

Janet Goff
Executive Director of Operations
2100 N. Carrolton Drive
Muncie, IN 47304